This Book Belongs To:

Rory Buehler

THE YOUNG
DANCER

Dancing together

String and scissors
for repairs

An attitude

Folk dancing

Standing in
fifth position

Learning to tie
shoe ribbons

THE YOUNG
DANCER

DARCEY
BUSSELL

with
Patricia Linton

An advanced jump

Flat leather shoes

Thread and shoe ribbons

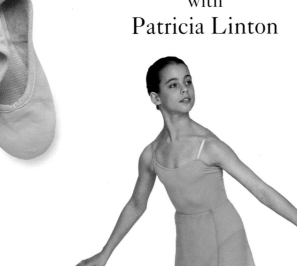

On pointe

Making up

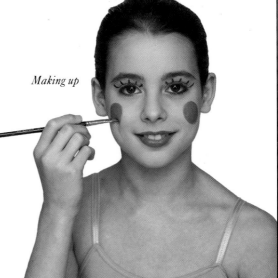

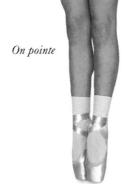

Putting on a performance

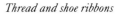

DK

A DK PUBLISHING BOOK

Project Editor Louise Pritchard **Art Editor** Carole Orbell

US Assistant Editor Camela Decaire

Special Photography Liz Mcaulay and John Garrett

Production Catherine Semark

Deputy Editorial Director Sophie Mitchell
Deputy Art Director Miranda Kennedy

The Young Dancers:
Georgina Broadhurst, Lara Glew, Robert Gravenor, Elizabeth Holliday, Oliver Lewis,
Nandita Shankardass, Lisa Todd, Anna Totesaut, Alex Whitley

First American Edition 1994
6 8 10 9 7

Published in the United States by DK Publishing, Inc.
95 Madison Avenue, New York, New York 10016

Copyright © 1994 Dorling Kindersley Limited, London

Visit us on the World Wide Web at http://www.dk.com

Library of Congress Cataloging-in-Publication Data

Bussell, Darcey
  The young dancer/Darcey Bussell, Patricia Linton – 1st
American ed.
  p. cm.
  Includes index.
  ISBN 1-56458-468-2
  1. Ballet dancing–Juvenile literature   [1. Ballet dancing.]
I. Linton, Patricia. II. Title
GV1787.5.B88 1994   93-36790
792.8–dc20   CIP
                                                      AC

Color reproduction by Colourscan, Singapore
Printed and bound in Italy

Contents

To all young dancers

" I FIRST started going to ballet classes on Saturday mornings when I was only five years old. But I never thought of it as a career until I was thirteen, and then I still had years of training ahead of me. Sometimes ballet classes can seem repetitive and too strenuous, and it takes real dedication to persevere. But the rewards of finally performing are truly amazing. Dance is one of the few arts in which we ourselves are the material, and every dancer becomes the ultimate artist, creating his or her own work. I hope you enjoy reading this book, and that it inspires you to persevere. Don't forget your dream of performing! *"*

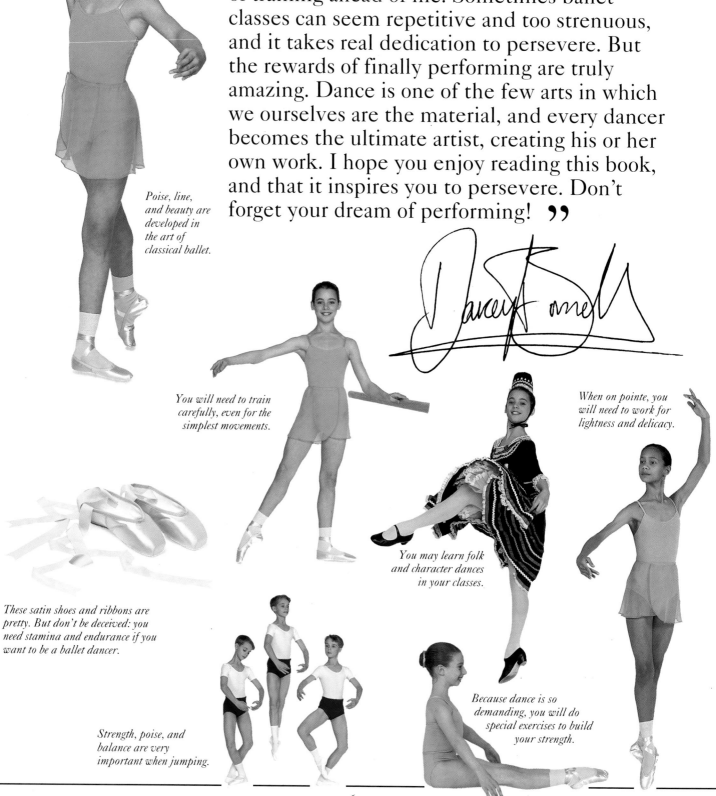

Poise, line, and beauty are developed in the art of classical ballet.

You will need to train carefully, even for the simplest movements.

When on pointe, you will need to work for lightness and delicacy.

You may learn folk and character dances in your classes.

These satin shoes and ribbons are pretty. But don't be deceived: you need stamina and endurance if you want to be a ballet dancer.

Strength, poise, and balance are very important when jumping.

Because dance is so demanding, you will do special exercises to build your strength.

It is fun to work together. Helping someone else with their technique will help you develop your own.

The tradition of ballet

As an art, ballet in Europe originated in the 15th and 16th centuries in lavish court entertainments, known as masques. Through the work of dedicated teachers, its traditions have been handed down to students year after year, and developed by each generation. In order to dance beautifully, you need to feel and understand the tradition of ballet. Try to learn and appreciate it for yourself and feel that you are a part of it. Your dancing will grow and develop in feeling if you know about other arts, too, such as music and painting. Sensitivity to different forms of beauty, including that of nature, can only make you more sensitive to beauty in ballet.

Carlotta Grisi was one of the greatest ballerinas of the Romantic period – the first half of the 19th century.

Pas de deux requires years of specialized training. If you start with simple poses such as this one, the complex poses of the great masterpieces will eventually be clear.

When you choreograph your own ballets, your imagination is free to explore music and ideas. Creating a theatrical presentation can be inspiring as well as great fun.

Ballet today

The love of ballet is not confined to a particular place or time. People all over the world appreciate it and enjoy its lightness and grace. Its movements speak straight to the heart and eye. Because ballet is a living art that is always developing, today's dancers and choreographers create new ballets as well as restage the classics. I gain great pleasure from dancing and enjoy the fact that I am still learning all the time.

I have been able to dance in great ballets such as Swan Lake *because of good training and hard work.*

Getting ready for class

O N STAGE, especially in older ballets, costumes are full and lavish, but daily practice clothes are quite different. In a ballet class, where you study and practice before going on to perform, you will concentrate on form, line, and movement. The clothes that you wear are designed with this in mind. They are practical and uncluttered. You must be able to move and stretch easily, and your teacher must be able to see exactly what you are doing.

Boys generally keep their hair short to avoid having it fall in their eyes.

Extra elastic

Pins and barrettes for keeping hair neat

Small sewing kit for last-minute repairs

Extra ribbon

Supply box
It is important to be well organized and arrive at class with everything you need. Many students find it useful to carry a box in which to keep extra supplies.

Girls' clothes
A simple leotard is the best thing for girls to wear in class. Sometimes they may wear a short skirt over it. It is best to wear socks, not tights, until the age of about eleven or twelve. With bare legs, a teacher can see that all muscles are working correctly when learning the movements. Girls can wear leather, canvas, or satin flat shoes with elastic or ribbons. Later, they can wear satin pointe shoes with ribbons.

Satin flat shoes

Boys' clothes
To start with, many boys wear trunks over a sleeveless tanktop or leotard, and socks. Later, they can wear tights with a leotard or T-shirt, or a unitard. Boys wear leather or canvas shoes with elastic.

Canvas shoes

Neat hair
Make sure your hair is tidy and off your face for your class. For girls, it is ideal if hair is long enough to put up – about shoulder length. Ask a friend to help you put your hair up if you find it difficult to begin with. If your hair is too short to put up, just pin or tie it back securely.

Sewing on the elastic
To find the right place to sew on your elastic or ribbon, fold the heel of your shoe in. The crease that is made at the side of the shoe is about the right place. Angle the elastic or ribbon slightly toward the toe and sew about $1/2$ in. into the shoe. Sew one ribbon in each side, or measure the elastic over your foot and allow another $1/2$ in. to sew in the other side.

Do not sew through the drawstring.

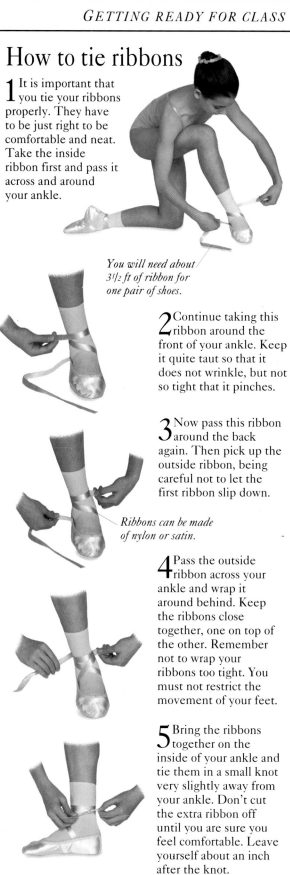

Remove all jewelry
Do not wear jewelry in class. Earrings are dangerous and a watch might scratch someone, or snag tights or leotards.

How to tie ribbons

1 It is important that you tie your ribbons properly. They have to be just right to be comfortable and neat. Take the inside ribbon first and pass it across and around your ankle.

You will need about 3¹/₂ ft of ribbon for one pair of shoes.

2 Continue taking this ribbon around the front of your ankle. Keep it quite taut so that it does not wrinkle, but not so tight that it pinches.

3 Now pass this ribbon around the back again. Then pick up the outside ribbon, being careful not to let the first ribbon slip down.

Ribbons can be made of nylon or satin.

4 Pass the outside ribbon across your ankle and wrap it around behind. Keep the ribbons close together, one on top of the other. Remember not to wrap your ribbons too tight. You must not restrict the movement of your feet.

Alternative outfits
A tutu may be suitable for a girl to wear on a special occasion. Tutus that you see professional dancers wearing on stage take a long time to make because they are specially sewn and fitted. You can buy a ready-made one from a specialty shop if you have a special performance.

Footwear
It is best to go to a store that specializes in dance shoes to have your shoes fitted properly. Shoes should not be too loose or too tight. They should fit like a glove. Your feet, especially your toes, must be able to work freely while the shoes feel quite snug and secure. Unless your teacher asks you to buy more, only buy one pair of shoes at a time because your feet are always growing.

Use the drawstring to adjust the fit around the top of your shoe. Then tuck in the ends.

5 Bring the ribbons together on the inside of your ankle and tie them in a small knot very slightly away from your ankle. Don't cut the extra ribbon off until you are sure you feel comfortable. Leave yourself about an inch after the knot.

Darning pointe shoes
Don't buy pointe shoes until your teacher asks you to. This will not be until you have studied hard for several years. When you do buy them, you can make them last longer by darning the ends.

Putting shoes away
Check to see if your shoes need to be cleaned or repaired after every class. Fold each shoe neatly, then wrap any ribbons around and tuck in the ends. Keep all your dance shoes together in a bag.

6 Tuck in the knot and the ends to leave the ribbons looking neat and tidy. Pieces of ribbon that escape while you are dancing are often called "pigs' ears."

Starting ballet

Mirrors help you check your position.

B ALLET BEGAN in the Italian courts of the 15th century. The princes put on lavish spectacles that included poetry, music, singing, and dancing. Ballet grew as a separate dance form, and set steps and professional ballet dancers began to appear in the 17th century. King Louis XIV of France was himself a keen dancer, and France became the first center of the ballet world, establishing French as the language of ballet to this day. Ballet is an art that is beautifully expressive and dramatic. It can bring every emotion from humor to sorrow alive. But you will begin by studying rules that have been laid down over the centuries, slowly building a vocabulary of steps before you can perform. This will be hard work, but also rewarding; you will be entering a rich and fulfilling tradition.

Studios
Ballet studios can be any shape or size. There should be a barre around the walls for you to hold on to during the exercises at the beginning of class. The floor may be made of wood or vinyl. The surface of some studio floors is specially made to "give" a little as you jump. This is more comfortable to work on.

Dedicated training
To become a professional ballet dancer you will need determination, strength, a good teacher, and whole-hearted dedication. Even now that I am a ballerina, I still need to discipline myself to a daily training routine.

Early exercises
In your first classes, you will learn ballet steps slowly and carefully. You will also learn various movements based on natural actions, such as walking, running, skipping, and jumping, to help you develop coordination and musicality.

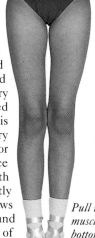

If there are two barres, use the one that is most comfortable for you.

Keep your shoulders down and open.

Strengthening your feet
This is a good exercise to do before class to warm up your feet and ankles. It helps you gain flexibility in your feet and down the backs of your legs.

Move with the music
During class, a pianist will work closely with your teacher. You must learn to feel the music and express what you feel in the way you move. Musicality is vital in a dancer.

Placement
In classical ballet your body needs to be correctly placed to help you find the necessary light and lifted qualities. In this preparatory exercise for placement, face the barre with your hands lightly on it, your elbows relaxed and slightly in front of your body.

Flex and stretch your feet, keeping a straight line through your legs.

Pull up the muscles in your bottom, legs, and tummy.

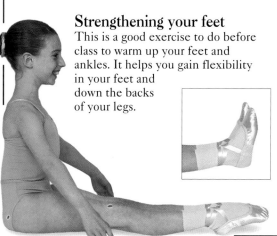

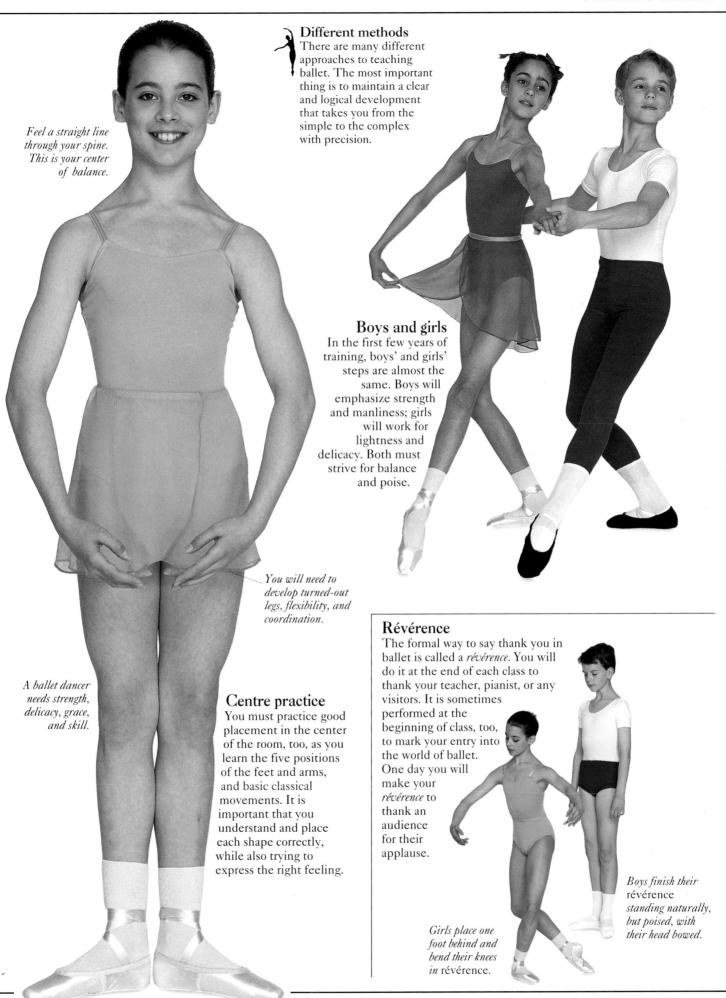

Feel a straight line through your spine. This is your center of balance.

Different methods
There are many different approaches to teaching ballet. The most important thing is to maintain a clear and logical development that takes you from the simple to the complex with precision.

Boys and girls
In the first few years of training, boys' and girls' steps are almost the same. Boys will emphasize strength and manliness; girls will work for lightness and delicacy. Both must strive for balance and poise.

You will need to develop turned-out legs, flexibility, and coordination.

A ballet dancer needs strength, delicacy, grace, and skill.

Centre practice
You must practice good placement in the center of the room, too, as you learn the five positions of the feet and arms, and basic classical movements. It is important that you understand and place each shape correctly, while also trying to express the right feeling.

Révérence
The formal way to say thank you in ballet is called a *révérence*. You will do it at the end of each class to thank your teacher, pianist, or any visitors. It is sometimes performed at the beginning of class, too, to mark your entry into the world of ballet. One day you will make your *révérence* to thank an audience for their applause.

Boys finish their révérence *standing naturally, but poised, with their head bowed.*

Girls place one foot behind and bend their knees in révérence.

11

Basic positions

EVERY NEW STEP you will learn makes use of these basic positions. You will use them at the beginning and end of movements, and in passing from one movement to another. All dancers use these exact shapes and positions to perform the most beautiful and expressive series of steps. It is vital that you understand the five positions of both the feet and arms well, and can perform them correctly with perfect confidence. As you get older, and your classes become more complex, it will be difficult for you to correct mistakes in your basic work. Learning these basics correctly now will give you a great advantage.

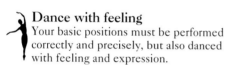

Dance with feeling
Your basic positions must be performed correctly and precisely, but also danced with feeling and expression.

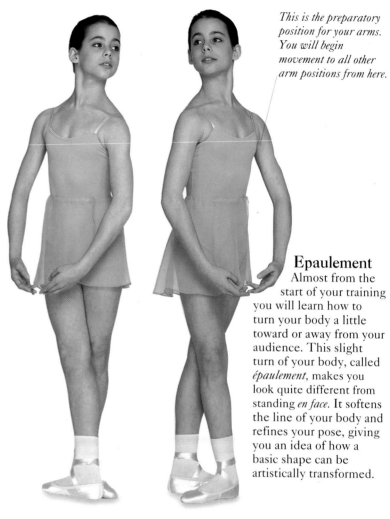

This is the preparatory position for your arms. You will begin movement to all other arm positions from here.

Epaulement
Almost from the start of your training you will learn how to turn your body a little toward or away from your audience. This slight turn of your body, called *épaulement*, makes you look quite different from standing *en face*. It softens the line of your body and refines your pose, giving you an idea of how a basic shape can be artistically transformed.

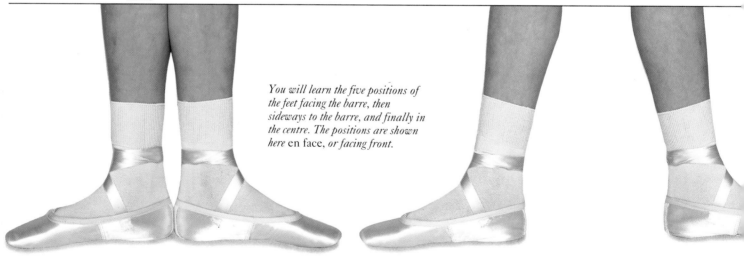

You will learn the five positions of the feet facing the barre, then sideways to the barre, and finally in the centre. The positions are shown here en face, *or facing front.*

Positions of the feet

First position
With your heels touching, turn each leg out from the hip, moving your toes to the side. At first you may not be able to turn out very far. Don't try to force your feet – it will improve with practice and hard work.

Second position
Keep your toes in the same line as first position, but place your feet apart. The space between your heels should be approximately the length of one foot. Be careful not to roll your feet forward, putting too much weight on your big toes.

Positions of the arms

Keep your arm just in front of the line of your shoulders.

1 Hold your arms in front in an oval shape. Your hands should continue the line of your arms. Curve your fingers, especially the third, and relax your thumbs toward your palms.

Move smoothly from one position to the next.

2 Open your arms wide, but keep them in front of your shoulders and slightly rounded. Be careful not to drop your elbows and try to keep your fingers delicate and soft.

3 Hold one arm curved in front of you and the other arm out to the side. To help you keep the right shape, imagine that something is gently supporting your little fingers and your elbows.

4 Take one arm up and hold it in a graceful curve, slightly in front of your head. Your other arm should be out to the side, also gently rounded. In all positions, remember to keep your tummy muscles pulled up as well as the muscles of your buttocks. Keep your back straight and your shoulders down and open.

5 Take both arms up and hold them in an oval shape, framing your face. Do not let your shoulders lift with your arms. Without looking up, you should be aware of your fingers, slightly in front of your head.

Pull up your body
Always keep your body well lifted, or "pulled up," and you will find it easier to turn out your legs from your hip joints. It will also help you look and feel light and secure.

The distance between your feet should be about the length of one of your own feet.

Third position
Cross one foot halfway in front of the other. Don't forget that it is not just your feet working. Keep your legs turned out and your body lifted. Your weight should be balanced evenly on both legs.

Fourth position
This position can be either crossed or open. For crossed, shown here, place one foot exactly in front of the other with a space between them. Uncross your legs, putting your heels in line but keeping the space, to perform the open position.

Fifth position
You will study this position when your feet and legs have become strong enough to hold the other positions correctly. It requires good turnout to be performed well. Stand with your feet fully crossed and touching each other firmly.

Pliés and Relevés

T HE ORDER of the exercises that you do in your ballet class has been developed over generations to give your body and mind the right preparation for dancing. At first your class will be quite slow and simple, but simple does not mean mechanical or like a robot. Even simple steps should be done artistically, intelligently, and musically. Each step has its own quality that gives it a life of its own. *Pliés* (*plier* meaning to bend or fold) and *relevés* (*relever* meaning to raise) are the first movements you will learn. They are also the foundation of almost every movement in classical dance.

Preparation of the arm

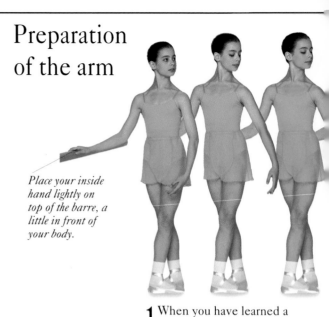

Place your inside hand lightly on top of the barre, a little in front of your body.

1 When you have learned a movement facing the barre, you will also perform it sideways. Begin with your free arm in preparatory position. During the musical introduction before the exercise begins, take a breath to lift and lighten your body. With this breath, slightly open your free arm starting with your fingertips.

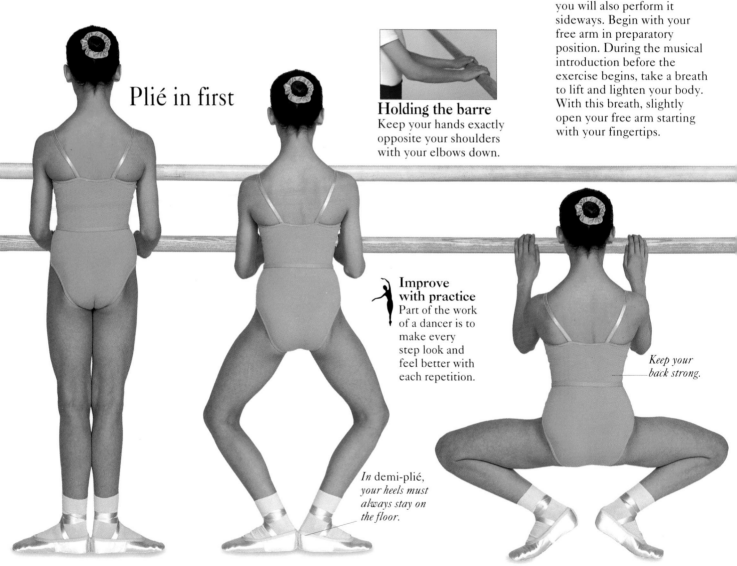

Plié in first

Holding the barre
Keep your hands exactly opposite your shoulders with your elbows down.

Improve with practice
Part of the work of a dancer is to make every step look and feel better with each repetition.

In demi-plié, *your heels must always stay on the floor.*

Keep your back strong.

1 *Pliés* are ideal for preparing your body at the start of class. Stand facing the barre with your legs stretched, your shoulders and hips level, and your body lifted.

2 Bend your knees and try to increase the turnout in the upper part of your legs. Without taking your heels off the ground, go as far as your ankles will allow.

3 To continue into a *grand plié*, gradually let your heels lift a little as you continue to bend your knees until your thighs are parallel with the floor. Coming up, replace your heels as soon as you can without forcing them.

Pliés in the centre

It is harder to balance and hold your turnout without the barre. Even so, you will soon try each new step during centre practice. Feel your muscles holding the shape exactly as you did at the barre. *Grand pliés* in fourth and fifth positions are even more difficult and you will not be asked to try these until you are quite advanced.

Grand plié in fourth

Grand plié in fifth

Relevé in first position

1 This movement will help you develop strength in your legs and feet. Place your weight evenly over both feet.

2 Smoothly lift both your heels off the floor at the same time. Keep your knees taut and try hard to hold your turnout. Keep your stomach and back muscles strong.

3 Continue to rise to *demi-pointe*. Think about "gathering" yourself up and feeling your center of balance. Slowly lower your heels. Feel a line through the center of each foot so that you work both evenly.

It is dangerous to lean on either your big or little toes.

2 Pass your hand back through preparatory to first position. Following your hand with your eyes, open your arm to second position.

Plié in second

Never let your knees fall inward. They must always look over your toes.

Work both legs equally.

Keep very straight as your knees bend and stretch.

1 This exercise will help you gain strength and elasticity in your muscles. Stand in second position. Feel your weight spread evenly over both legs.

2 Bend slowly and smoothly into a *demi-plié*, working your turnout as much as you can. For stability and control it is important to feel a line through the length of your spine and through the top of your head. This is your center of balance, or axis.

3 Bend your knees more, into a *grand plié*, and this time keep your heels on the floor throughout. Come up again as carefully as you went down. A *plié* should be beautifully balanced and smooth.

Battement tendu

THE WORD *battement* literally means "beat" or "beating." In ballet the word is used to define a whole family of movements where the working leg opens and closes. There are different kinds of *battement*, and each has its own value and character. When you perform them in class you will usually repeat one movement several times. At first you will practice slowly, facing the barre, but this exercise is also part of centre practice.

Battement tendu jeté
This exercise will help you feel light and full of energy. *Jeté* means "thrown," but in *battement tendu jeté*, throw your leg only a few inches off the ground. Fix a point in the air with your toes before closing your legs.

Battement tendu
This exercise helps you improve your turnout, warm up your legs, and build strength for the work ahead. *Tendu* means "stretched." You must feel the bottom of your foot stretch out along the floor.

Keep your head and shoulders poised and do not strain.

Keep your back square.

Battement tendu derrière
Derrière means "behind." Slide your leg straight backward from first or fifth position, leading with your toes.

Turn out your thigh as much as you can.

Battement tendu à la seconde
This is done to the side. Slide your leg out sideways, trying to form a straight line through your stretched knee, instep, and toes.

Battement tendu devant
Devant means "in front." Lead with your heel and continue with your toes.

Keep your knee straight as you open your leg.

Keep your knee turned out.

When you have stretched your leg out fully, carefully close it again to the original position. Lower your whole foot gradually to the floor.

Your supporting leg must work, too. Try to keep it still, straight, and turned out. This will help the rest of your body stay balanced.

When your heel lifts off the floor, continue with your toes until you reach your maximum stretch.

Battement tendu soutenu

You will later find that the basic *battement tendu* can be developed in a wide variety of ways. In *soutenu*, your supporting leg goes through a *demi-plié* as your stretched working leg slides out.

Feel a straight line from the top of your head to the tip of your toes.

This is a good exercise for strength, flexibility, control, and coordination.

Keep your back very square and remember to hold your turnout.

Advanced positions

When you are more advanced, you may finish your barre exercises, including *battement tendu* and *battement tendu jeté*, with a special pose or position. These varied shapes follow exact rules that you will learn step by step.

It is important to keep your shoulders and hips level.

Try to feel graceful with a beautiful line from your neck and the top of your back through to the tips of your toes.

Don't forget
It is important to feel confident at one level before you move on to the next.

Your supporting knee should be over your toes.

Rond de jambe

1 *Rond de jambe parterre* is a semi-circular movement made on the floor with the working leg. It will help you feel the mobility of your hip joints. You can circle your leg either *en dehors* (outward), or *en dedans* (inward), as here. Slide your foot backward, as in *battement tendu*.

2 To begin with, move your arm and leg together. Then hold your arm in second position while continuing to circle forward with your leg only. Turn your head to look straight forward.

3 When learning, pause slightly in each position to check your form before moving on to the next. Keep your legs turned out and beautifully stretched.

4 Move your leg freely and smoothly, so that your toes glide across the floor. Keep your supporting leg turned out and your stomach pulled in.

5 As you continue to circle your leg from behind again, it is important to keep your knee and foot stretched. You cannot look at it, so you must feel that your leg is correctly positioned.

6 During a *rond de jambe*, try to maintain your center of balance, with your shoulders and hips level. As you circle your leg, your foot must be fully stretched and no weight should rest on your working toes.

Battement fondu

Y OU CAN LEARN many things from practicing *battement fondu*, especially about how ballet and music work together. You must listen to the music as you dance – your movements should always reflect it and express its rhythm and feeling. *Battement fondu* is a melting, flowing movement in which the legs work together smoothly, exercising your strength and turnout, as well as coordination and timing. The ability to move softly and expressively will help you join different steps together seamlessly, and also help you coordinate your jumps as you advance.

If you work carefully, little by little you will develop your turnout, strength, and suppleness.

Battement fondu to 45°
You can open your working leg in any direction at the end of *battement fondu*. From *cou de pied derrière*, you can stretch up and out to 45°. It is important to feel a straight line pulled up through your supporting leg to keep your thigh well turned out. Turn your front hand palm down, gently following the line of your arm.

Battement fondu to 90°
You will gradually be able to lift your leg higher. Extend your working leg behind you in a beautiful sweeping movement. Your body will tilt slightly forward, but hold the middle of your back upright. Keep your neck gently curved and your front arm looking relaxed.

When you have mastered the basic fondu, you may try battement fondu *on* demi-pointe.

How to dance a battement fondu

At first you will learn *battement fondu* with your working toe on the floor, opening your leg to the side, and then to the front and back. Your next step will be to reach to 45° in each direction, with your supporting foot flat on the floor. After a lot of practice, you will learn to rise to *demi-pointe* as you extend your working leg. Finally, you will extend to 90° or more, rising to *demi-* or even full pointe. Advanced dancers can use all these possibilities in fascinating and expressive ways.

Begin by looking at your fingertips.

Always hold the barre lightly. Don't grip with your hand: this will spoil your placement and posture and you will find it harder to work on your balance.

1 This is a *battement fondu* to 45° in second position. Start by standing in fifth, with your arm in preparatory position. During the musical introduction, take a breath to calm and prepare your whole body and mind for the movement.

Your hand should be soft and delicate.

2 Bring your arm carefully back through preparatory position, following the movement with your eyes. At the same time, lift your working foot smoothly off the floor, keeping your heel well forward, and begin to bend both knees together.

Wait until the moment that your toes leave the floor before gradually bending your supporting knee.

Sur le cou de pied

This literally means "on the neck of the foot." In this position, your working foot is placed in a certain way on your other ankle. It can be flexed naturally, wrapped around, or fully stretched in *cou de pied*. The position forms the basis of many different steps. You can take it up smoothly, quickly, strongly, or lightly. Your supporting leg can be in a *demi-plié*, on a flat foot, or on *demi-pointe*.

Keep your heel forward.

With your knee and thigh turned out properly, this position is very useful for improving your turnout.

Devant
Here your supporting leg is in a *demi-plié* while your working foot is fully stretched. Place the tip of your toe exactly on your ankle bone.

Derrière
You can take up a *cou de pied* position with your supporting leg straight and your working foot placed *derrière*. Remember to hold the turnout of your working thigh.

Wrapped around
When placed *devant*, your working foot may be "wrapped around" your supporting ankle, with your heel toward the front and your toes behind.

As you open your leg sideways, look straight ahead.

Finish with your arm in second position.

Open your shoulders and keep them level with your hips.

Look gracefully into your hand.

Hold your arm precisely but softly in first position.

Remember to hold your turnout all the time.

5 Your legs should straighten simultaneously as your arm and leg arrive in second position. Stretch as tall and long as you can, while still maintaining your center of balance. It is important to keep well pulled up on your supporting side. Reach with your toes to an exact, invisible point in the air – this will help you capture a precise shape.

3 As you *demi-plié* on one leg, bring your other foot into a *cou de pied* position, making sure your foot is pointed. "Melt" to your deepest point and increase the turnout of both legs as much as you can. Your knees should look over your toes and your hips should stay level.

4 Open your working leg at the same time as you slowly stretch your supporting leg. Your legs must work together. Begin to carry your free arm to second position. Keep the movement smooth and steady and stretch up through the length of your spine to feel light and lifted.

Don't forget
From start to finish, a *battement fondu* is always smooth and elastic, whatever the speed or rhythm of the music.

Further exercises

THE LANGUAGE of ballet is rich and varied. On stage you will have to change quickly from small, fast steps to smooth, graceful ones. You therefore need to get used to different ways and speeds of moving. The development and preparation of barre exercises will help you. The exercises follow a logical pattern, designed to make sure that, while gaining strength, you do not overwork your muscles. After the smooth elasticity of *battement fondu*, you will be ready for some fast work close to the ground, such as *battement frappé* and *petit battement*. Following *rond de jambe en l'air*, you will be fully warmed up and ready for big movements to 90° or higher. These can be slow and sustained, like *développé* and *relevé lent*, or fast and sweeping, like *grand battement*.

Petit battement

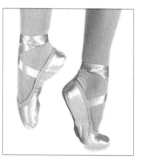

1 *Petit battement* means "small beat." This movement will help your lower leg move quickly and freely. Your working foot can be pointed, flexed, or wrapped around in *cou de pied.*

2 Open your toes a little to the side, moving freely in the knee. Keep your thigh still and turned out.

3 Bring your working foot to *cou de pied derrière.* On the next beat, return your foot to the original position. Make your beats strong and accurate. Your teacher will tell you how many to do.

Battement frappé

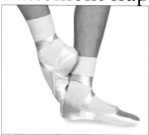

1 *Frapper* means "to strike." This movement is fast and energetic. It will help you develop strength and flexibility in your lower leg. Your working foot can be pointed, flexed, or wrapped around in *cou de pied.*

2 Open your lower leg quickly and strongly to second position, keeping your thigh turned out and still. At first, put an equal accent on opening and closing. Later, you will extend to a slightly higher position and "strike" the floor as you extend your leg.

Développé

Place your hand correctly on the barre.

1 *Battement développé* is a big unfolding movement of *adage.* It helps develop strength, balance, and control, and requires good flexibility. For *développé à la seconde,* start in fifth with your working arm in preparatory position.

Don't let this arm move.

2 Breathe, and gently open the lower part of your arm sideways from preparatory position, starting with your fingertips. Look elegantly at your hand as it opens. Bring your arm back through preparatory position as the exercise begins.

3 Holding your turnout as you move, lift your working leg through *cou de pied.* Make sure your toes and instep are very stretched and your heel is well forward. Lift your arm to first position.

4 Slide your toe up to *retiré* position. Take it right up to your knee and keep increasing your turnout as you go. The unfolding should be clear and light, not dull and heavy. Try not to let this look difficult.

Keep your supporting leg straight and your body lifted.

5 Extend your leg smoothly, slowly straightening your knee as you open your arm to second position. Keep your back square and your shoulders level. Hold your leg very still in the open position, then lower slowly and carefully to fifth position.

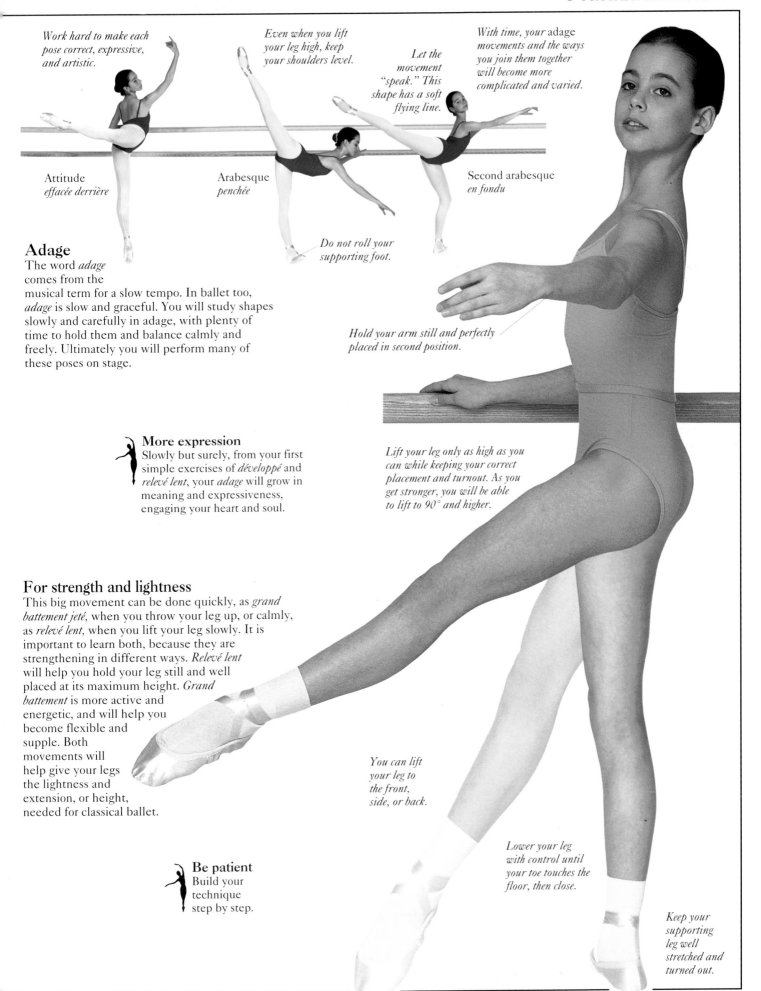

Work hard to make each pose correct, expressive, and artistic.

Even when you lift your leg high, keep your shoulders level.

Let the movement "speak." This shape has a soft flying line.

With time, your adage movements and the ways you join them together will become more complicated and varied.

Attitude
effacée derrière

Arabesque
penchée

Second arabesque
en fondu

Do not roll your supporting foot.

Adage

The word *adage* comes from the musical term for a slow tempo. In ballet too, *adage* is slow and graceful. You will study shapes slowly and carefully in adage, with plenty of time to hold them and balance calmly and freely. Ultimately you will perform many of these poses on stage.

Hold your arm still and perfectly placed in second position.

More expression

Slowly but surely, from your first simple exercises of *développé* and *relevé lent*, your *adage* will grow in meaning and expressiveness, engaging your heart and soul.

Lift your leg only as high as you can while keeping your correct placement and turnout. As you get stronger, you will be able to lift to 90° and higher.

For strength and lightness

This big movement can be done quickly, as *grand battement jeté*, when you throw your leg up, or calmly, as *relevé lent*, when you lift your leg slowly. It is important to learn both, because they are strengthening in different ways. *Relevé lent* will help you hold your leg still and well placed at its maximum height. *Grand battement* is more active and energetic, and will help you become flexible and supple. Both movements will help give your legs the lightness and extension, or height, needed for classical ballet.

You can lift your leg to the front, side, or back.

Lower your leg with control until your toe touches the floor, then close.

Be patient

Build your technique step by step.

Keep your supporting leg well stretched and turned out.

Stretching and strengthening

BALLET IS AN ART that will make extreme demands on your body. To be a dancer you must be supple, strong, and well coordinated. You need to be able to jump, have good turnout, and the strength to lift your legs up lightly and easily. As you advance, the ever increasing physical demands require special exercises that will play an important supporting role in your training. But remember that ballet is first and foremost an art. So when you stretch or do other special exercises, try to imagine how they will help you with the balletic movements you are also learning.

Learning to lift
This exercise will help you feel the muscles in your buttocks and the backs of your thighs. It will strengthen your back, too. When you are lying on the floor it is easier to feel if you are straining your shoulders or twisting your hips as you lift your leg behind you. Carefully correct your mistakes now in order to ready yourself for arabesques.

Bending on stage
Some ballets require more flexibility than others! This is a pose from the ballet *Medea*, performed by the Dance Theatre of Harlem.

Your head and hands should always complete the picture. Place them correctly and elegantly as you stretch sideways, and keep your head and body in perfect alignment.

When you are sitting down, your legs do not have to support your weight. You will therefore find it easier to concentrate on your back, neck, and arms.

Stretching in a sitting position
There are many stretching exercises you can do sitting down. These will help you develop the right sort of suppleness, and pinpoint areas that might be a little stiff. When you bend sideways, you are stretching the muscles on the side you lean away from. You should be able to feel a gentle, painless stretch.

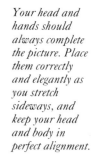

Be careful
There is a big difference between sustained effort and force! Don't force your body into shapes it does not want to make.

Professional dancers have their own special sequences of warm-up exercises. Your teacher will help you work out exercises for your feet, tummy, and back muscles. You should always warm up before class.

Warming up

As a professional dancer, I rehearse every day and perform on many evenings, too. I have to be light on my feet and sometimes have to move very fast. My body must be perfectly tuned to withstand this work. I am therefore careful to keep it flexible by warming up properly.

The splits

You should only do stretching exercises like the splits after your barre work or at the end of a class. Your muscles must be very warm or you will strain them. Getting flexible enough to do the splits may take several months, or more, of practice. Don't twist your hips or awkwardly force your body.

Keep breathing

Breathe naturally with the movement of each exercise. Rhythmical breathing helps with the flow of movement and therefore with its range and suppleness.

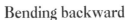

Bending forward

Bend forward gradually and smoothly, keeping your legs taut and turned out. Lower your arm naturally as you bend, and try hard not to sway backward with your hips. You will feel a stretch through the backs of your legs.

Bending backward

Hold your arm in a curve above your head. Hold your back and your stomach muscles strongly. Bend your shoulders and upper back first. You can only go back a little way with the top of your back, then your lower back will take over the movement.

Going farther

Be careful to control the line of your head and arm as you go farther back. You should keep them in the same position. Bend as far as you can without forcing and don't let your hips push forward. Breathe out as you bend back. Breathe in to help you return to the upright position.

Using all your muscles

Your exercises have to be well balanced. Don't overwork one group of muscles at the expense of others. After stretching sideways, you should bend backward and forward. Keep both hands on your knees.

Extend and lengthen your spine as you bend back. Feel as if the front of your rib cage is lifting up from within.

Always feel the straight line of your spine before you move.

Curl your head down toward your knees, starting with the top of your neck, and continuing down to the bottom of your back. When you come up, reverse the movement, uncurling from the base of your back first.

Using your arms

A VITAL PART of the art of dancing is the way dancers use their arms. This is called *port de bras*, which literally means "carriage of the arms." Although you learn arm movements separately, you should not think of them in isolation. Your arms should join harmoniously with the movements of your body. At first the forms are simple. Later, when you have learned to combine them with bends and turns of the body, *port de bras* will be involved in everything you do. Different schools have their own particular patterns and sequences for teaching *port de bras*, but all aim at the same goals of finesse, harmony, and expression.

How to hold your hands

Basic hand position
Place your hand so that it looks natural and relaxed. Keep your fingers delicately and softly grouped.

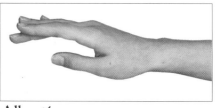

Allongé
This position is a nuance and a refinement of the basic position. Open your fingers and gently turn your palm downward.

Advanced port de bras

Lift your eyes and then follow your hand.

Listen very carefully to the music and breathe naturally, feeling the rise and fall of each movement.

You will need supervision
You will not learn this sort of *port de bras* until you are advanced, and only with the guidance of your teacher.

1 This is an advanced *port de bras* sequence because it involves bending your body forward, sideways, and backward as well as using your arms. Start in fifth position, *épaulement croisé*, with your arms in preparatory position. During the musical introduction, take your arms up, passing through first position.

2 Lift up and then over as you bend forward smoothly.

3 Continue bending forward. Lower your head and bring your hands together. Try to let the movements flow smoothly and without tension.

4 Begin to come up smoothly and naturally. Keep your hands carefully placed and look at them. Hold your shoulders down and your hips still.

Keep your legs stretched and in a tight fifth position. Don't sway backward.

Simple port de bras

When you have learned the rules for the placement and posture of your arms, you are ready to start joining the shapes together. For this simple *port de bras* exercise, start in preparatory position, then bring your arms up, passing through first position. Let your head and eyes follow the smooth, free movement of your arms.

Keep your shoulders down and open.

Try to keep your body lifted and poised.

Arms used choreographically

On stage, you will use your arms to help you portray a wonderful range of characters and feelings. The exact movements will be determined by the choreographer of the ballet. Here, the Houston Ballet is performing *Serenade*, choreographed by George Balanchine.

Be guided by the music and feel its life within you as you move.

As your body bends, always remember to keep your legs strong and straight. Do not roll your ankles.

5 Bring your body up until you are standing upright again. Your arms should be elegantly curved in front in first position.

6 Still looking into your hands, turn slightly away from the audience. Keep your shoulders level and open and your hips still.

7 Raise your right arm and open your left as you start to bend smoothly backward. Follow your top arm around with your head and eyes, naturally and easily.

8 Bring your body upright as you gracefully change your arms to return to your starting position.

Classical ballet poses

THE BASIC POSES of classical ballet have been developed over centuries and form the structure on which the whole of ballet rests. There is a great variety of ways in which poses can be developed and performed, but, underneath the elaboration, the basic shapes are always recognizable. This is why it is important to learn them correctly from the beginning. Perform them with feeling, and above all, remember to involve your whole body, from your head and eyes to your toes and fingertips.

On stage
When you perform on stage, you will have to project your work differently according to your size and shape. Here, three dancers from The Royal Ballet take up a pose (*croisé devant* with both arms up) during the ballet *The Nutcracker*.

Ecarté devant
This position is set on the diagonal with your leg, arms, and head all on the same plane. Stand as if you were facing a corner of the front of the stage. Extend the leg nearest the audience to second position. Hold your downstage arm up and your other arm to the side. Keep your hips level and incline your body slightly away from the audience.

You incline your body differently in each pose. This is an important part of its line.

Croisé devant
This *croisé* pose is bright and clear. You usually learn *croisé* positions and poses first. For *croisé devant*, stretch the leg nearer the audience in front of you. Hold your upstage arm high and your other arm to the side. Look out to the audience and incline the top of your body very slightly back.

Ecarté derrière
This pose has a softer line. Extend the leg farthest from the audience to second position. Hold your upstage arm up and your other arm to the side. Incline your body and head slightly toward the audience and look down along the line of your arm. Your head is in profile.

The meanings
Ecarté means "separated"; *croisé* means "crossed"; *effacé* usually means "open" in ballet. Take these words and translate them into movement.

Keep your legs beautifully stretched.

In this pose, the line of your head crosses the line of your leg. To the audience, your whole body appears crossed.

Attitudes

There is a special pose in ballet called an attitude. It is a position on one leg, with the other lifted and bent either behind or in front of you. You will find that you use attitudes more in advanced work, in *adage* and in jumps, turns, and lifts. When you are young, you will learn it slowly and carefully in either *croisé* or *effacé* with the basic arm positions.

There is a delicate quality to the line of your head and neck.

Both of these attitudes are in croisé *positions.*

Keep your shoulders level. At 90° incline forward very slightly.

Correct alignment

This position is effacé devant parterre.

This diagram will help you see the particular direction of a movement and the amount of turn your body has to make for épaulement croisé *or* effacé.

Upstage (the back of the stage)

Downstage (the front of the stage)

To help you visualize the different positions of the body when you are learning, imagine that you are standing in the middle of a "star" of lines. You can then make sure your body is aligned correctly for *épaulement croisé* or *effacé*, or the *écarté* lines.

Place your arms carefully. Let your head and eyes complete the shape and don't forget to breathe in harmony with the movements.

Effacé devant

In *effacé* poses, the line of your body is open to the audience. For *effacé devant*, extend the leg farthest from the audience in front of you. Hold your downstage arm high and your other arm to the side. Lean your body slightly back, with your top arm gently framing your face. Look clearly upward and outward.

Effacé *poses should have an elusive flying quality.*

Use your whole body

The way you look must reflect the feeling of the pose. Give "spirit" to your pose by expressing the feeling you want with your eyes.

Croisé derrière

This is also a strong and direct pose. Extend the leg farthest from the audience behind you. Hold the same arm high and your other arm out to the side. Turn your head toward the audience. Keep your body straight.

Make sure your extended leg is exactly in front of or behind you, following the rules for battement tendu.

Effacé derrière

Stretch your downstage leg behind you. Hold the arm high on the same side and your other arm out to the side. Lean slightly forward, lift your head, and imagine you are flying.

27

Arabesques

O NE OF THE MOST BEAUTIFUL poses in ballet is the arabesque. The word originally described a form of ancient ornamental design composed of the flowing lines of branches, leaves, and scrolls. These were fancifully intertwined in complicated, yet beautifully balanced, patterns. In ballet, too, the dancer must be perfectly balanced, standing on one leg with the other well stretched out behind. The arms are extended in harmony with the legs, and the dancer forms a graceful curve from fingertips to toes.

Keep this leg beautifully stretched and turned out with a fully pointed foot.

Develop a basic shape
There are many different arabesques. You will learn the basic shapes first. Later, you will find that each one can be developed in a huge variety of ways to convey many different feelings and moods.

Try to visualize the shape you want to make with your leg and feel the line exactly.

Keep your shoulders down and open.

Your gaze should be steady and follow the line of your arm.

Hold your arms softly stretched.

Learning arabesques
To start with, you will learn an arabesque *parterre* to find the correct placement of your arms, legs, and body. The toes of your extended leg stay on the ground. Make sure there is no weight resting on them. Keep your body well lifted and try not to lean forward. To perform the arabesque shown here, stand on your right leg with your left arm forward and your right arm to the side. This is called an arabesque *croisée* because your legs appear crossed to the audience.

Arabesque to 90°
As you get stronger, you will be able to lift your leg higher. Try not to lean away from your center of balance as your leg goes up. Let your pelvis tilt forward slightly, but keep your stomach lifted and your shoulders back. Try to find the perfect shape and balance. Remember what it feels like, so that you can find it again.

More than just a step

As you progress, you will learn to use your head and eyes to make your arabesques even more artistic. Many dancers can perform the basic step, but only some can convey a special feeling and intensity. This is Miyako Yoshida performing a beautiful arabesque *penchée*. She is dancing with Petter Jacobsson for The Birmingham Royal Ballet in *Theme and Variations*.

Hold your hands palm down and softly stretched, with your fingertips leading the way.

Do not let your thumb drop too much and spoil the flowing line.

Placing your whole body

Whatever style of arabesque you are performing, try to feel the placement of the whole of your body. Keep your back strong and square and your working leg stretched and turned out. Turn both hands palm down and hold them softly. Your head should be poised with your eyes following the line of your arm. The angle of your palms and stretch of your arms should convey a feeling of flight to the audience.

Be careful not to drop your elbows.

When you start to study arabesques, hold your side arm slightly in front of your shoulder line. As you get older your teacher will ask you to open your side arm gradually at the shoulder joint.

Feel a perfect line softly flowing from fingertip to fingertip through your arms, back, and shoulders.

As you get stronger, try to keep the shoulder of your supporting side well lowered, and slightly drawn back.

Keep your supporting leg well turned out and as straight as possible.

Advanced arabesques

After years of practice you will try more difficult poses of arabesque, such as this one. With the same arm forward as your raised leg, turn your head to look over your front shoulder. Your back should be more strongly arched than in some other arabesques and the whole feeling should be more upright. This pose gives the impression of soaring upward like a bird.

It is important to keep the correct placement of your legs. Hold your hips level. Do not tip them toward the audience.

Croisé parterre

This arabesque is particularly expressive in the beautiful sweep of line through your back and neck as you turn your shoulders. Try to feel a line from the curve of your neck down through the center of your body as your arms and shoulders move.

Linking movements

A FTER YOU HAVE STUDIED most of the basic individual ballet steps and perfected your technique for each, you will begin to learn linking steps. These steps are as important as the positions they join, and you should work hard to understand their technique, rhythm, and timing. They will allow you to finally start dancing, performing sequences of steps. You will want to develop a sense of phrasing, accenting some steps more than others, to give your dancing vibrancy and drama. Your ability to portray a character or emotion on stage will depend on your mastery of linking steps.

Follow the movement of your hand with your eyes.

Don't forget
All exercises should be practiced to the right and to the left. Traveling steps should be practiced going backward, too.

It is a lovely feeling to skim across the floor swiftly with tiny little steps. Keep to a definite line. With practice, you will feel as if you are floating across the room.

Pas de couru

This is a run in any direction, and is a very useful joining step. *Pas de couru* can be a preparation for jumps, or it can join different types of steps together and make it easy for you to change direction. It can also be a little run in first position with your feet facing forward instead of turned out.

1 You can start *pas de couru* from various positions, sometimes from a *pas dégagé*, that is, with your foot pointed in an open position. Do a *battement tendu effacé devant* with a *demi-plié*.

Hold your arms as if they are resting on a beautiful full skirt.

2 Transfer your weight onto your opening leg smoothly and glide into a run.

Your hands can be high or low. Plan what you are going to do, then feel as delicate and free as a bird.

3 Take tiny steps as you travel forward. Imagine you are gently pushing your skirt away from you, or that you are gliding through a soft mist.

Temps lié

One of the most important linking movements is *temps lié*. You will use it to transfer smoothly from one position to another. Danced in the centre, it is an exercise complete in itself. It helps you develop the coordination of your whole body and your feeling for dance. Perform it as if you are pouring one movement into the other. *Temps lié* can become a more complicated exercise with bends of the body, high legs, and turns, and there may be slight differences of timing and style.

Try to get the details of each shape correct.

Incline your head to look into your hands.

Keep your body precisely placed and balanced.

1 *Temps lié en avant* travels forward. Start in fifth position with *épaulement croisé* and your arms low.

2 Take a small breath to free your arms, then *demi-plié*. Look into your hands.

3 Keep your back leg in *demi-plié* and stretch your other leg forward with a gliding feeling. Raise your arms in front of you to first position.

4 Continue to stretch your pointed toe forward, still on the floor. When you have reached the full stretch of your leg, transfer your weight very smoothly onto your front foot to the pose *croisé derrière*.

Hold your turnout as you transfer your weight.

Follow your hand with your eyes.

5 Close your back foot into fifth position *croisé*, turn *en face*, and *demi-plié*. Lower your top arm to first position, watching your hand as it moves.

6 Keep your back leg in *demi-plié* and stretch your other leg to the side. Open your arm.

7 Stretch your pointed toe along the floor, then transfer your weight immediately, but smoothly. Point the other foot to second position still facing front, and turn your hands palm down.

8 Close your legs in time to the music to fifth position *épaulement croisé*. Close your arms to preparatory position and look out to the audience.

Pas de bourrée

Practicing *pas de bourrée* will help you achieve neat and lively footwork. There are many forms of *pas de bourrée*, usually involving three quick changes of weight. You will learn them facing the barre and later, when you can perform them accurately, you will bring them into the centre. The extraordinary versatility of *pas de bourrée* means it can join many different types of steps together.

4 Finish this *pas de couru* in a position that flows naturally and artistically from the movement.

How to do a pas de bourrée

Start in *demi-plié* with your foot in *cou de pied derrière*. Gather yourself up quickly and lightly, and replace one foot with the other. Bring your arms to first position. Change feet again with a tiny step, lightly and exactly. Finish in *cou de pied derrière* in a *demi-plié* with *épaulement croisé*.

As you change your weight in pas de bourrée, *you never have two feet on the ground at the same time.*

Pirouettes

IN CLASSICAL BALLET there are many different ways of turning. As you advance, you will find that almost every movement can be danced *en tournant*, or going around. Pirouette means "to whirl," and you will learn to spin around on one leg. To prepare you for pirouettes, you will do simple exercises at the barre and in the centre, working on your balance and control. You will learn your first pirouettes with your raised leg in either *cou de pied* or *retiré* position. Later, you can extend your leg into any one of the big poses you have studied. These are called *grandes* pirouettes.

Spotting for a pirouette

Before you begin a pirouette, fix your eyes on a spot at head level. As you turn, keep your eyes fixed on that spot as long as possible, then quickly whip your head around and focus again. This not only creates some momentum, helping you complete your turn, it also helps to keep you from getting dizzy.

Do not let your elbows drop.

How to do a pirouette

1 Pirouettes turn *en dehors* and *en dedans*. Basic pirouettes usually begin in fourth, fifth, or second position. This is a preparation and pirouette from fourth position *en dehors*. Stand in fifth *croisé*, your arms in preparatory position, and your head turned to look over your front shoulder.

2 *Demi-plié*, lift your arms slightly, and look into your hands.

3 Spring into *retiré* position, your arms in first, to face the other corner. Find your center of balance, or axis, and hold it strongly.

4 Lower your raised leg to fourth position *croisé*. Open your arms with your hands *allongées*.

5 *Demi-plié* and push up into *retiré* position. Hold your arms in first and turn your body and legs together in one fixed shape.

Hold your arms steady, but not stiffly.

Don't let the heel of your supporting leg slip and turn in as you push up.

Keep your eyes level as you use your head.

Stay vertical throughout this type of pirouette. Hold your shoulders level and your hips square, and keep your body still.

6 Complete the pirouette firmly and calmly in a *demi-plié*. The finish is as important as the start. If you fall at the end of a turn, the audience will see that you are out of control.

Preparing for pirouettes

Don't try to turn before you can balance! Before you learn a proper pirouette you can practice doing lots of *relevé* preparations without a turn. This simple preparatory exercise will help you feel the correct line and balance of your body. It will also help you keep your body still and your legs taut and turned out.

Your head will come quickly around to the front in advance of your body.

Hold your back strongly, especially at the waist.

1 Stand *en face* in fifth position with one arm in front and the other to the side. *Demi-plié*, remembering to keep your feet placed evenly on the floor.

Keep your shoulders down and level.

2 *Relevé* strongly but calmly to *retiré* position. Feel your center line of balance and pull your body up through it to feel strong and controlled.

Hold your foot exactly in place as you turn.

Make sure your knees are looking over your toes as you close to fifth position, and do not roll forward.

3 Close your leg neatly behind to fifth position in a *demi-plié* with *épaulement croisé*. Feel composed when you finish, with your weight evenly on both feet.

Keep your supporting leg taut and both legs turned out throughout the pirouette.

First jumps

JUMPS ARE an important and exciting part of your class. Everything that you have worked on up to now has been preparing you for your first leaps. You can jump at different heights and speeds, on the spot or traveling. At first, boys and girls learn the same jumping steps, but as boys grow and develop more muscle, their steps become more complicated. They need to be strong and powerful as they jump whereas girls work for lightness, grace, and delicacy. In music, the word *allegro* means brisk and lively and these are the qualities you should strive for when jumping You will start with *petit allegro*, small neat steps. Later, when you become stronger, you will be able to jump higher. This is called *grand allegro*.

Understand the exercises
To help you have lovely stretched feet in the air, you must make sure you understand the exercises you do for your feet and insteps at the start of class.

Temps levé
The first and simplest jump you will learn is a *temps levé*. It is a jump on the spot, beginning and ending on two legs in a *demi-plié*. It can be done in any of the five positions of the feet. Later you will do a *temps levé* from one leg.

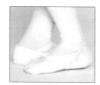

Preparation for a jump
Your preparation before a jump is important. It must be clear, rythmical, and exact. In the *demi-plié* before you spring up, press your whole foot, especially your heels, into the floor. This will give you the strength to push up into the air.

In the air
Be sure about what shape you are trying to make in the air. Fix your position exactly and stretch your legs and feet as much as you can. Remember to finish calmly and correctly.

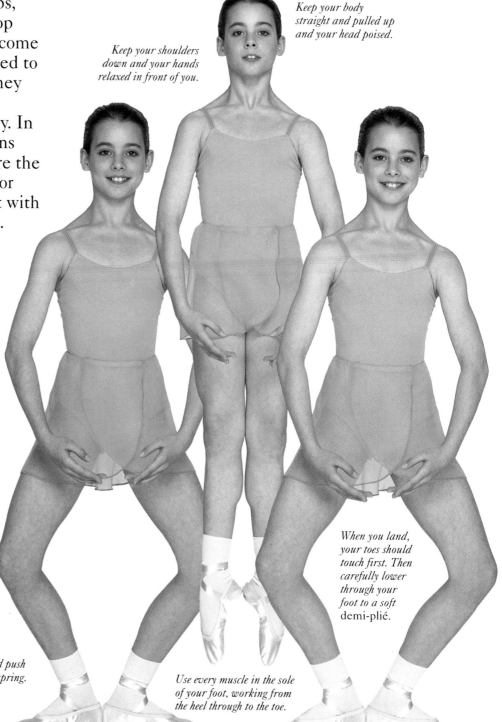

Keep your shoulders down and your hands relaxed in front of you.

Keep your body straight and pulled up and your head poised.

When you land, your toes should touch first. Then carefully lower through your foot to a soft demi-plié.

Hold your turnout and push from your heels like a spring.

Use every muscle in the sole of your foot, working from the heel through to the toe.

34

Echappée sautée

1 *Echapper* means to escape and an *échappée sautée* is a jump in which your legs open, or "escape" from one another, to a different position. You can do a *petite échappée* or a *grande échappée*. Start in fifth position in a *demi-plié*, ready to spring into the air. In *grande échappée* you will need to go into a deeper *demi-plié* for more power.

Petite échappée

Grande échappée

Move correctly
It is important to be very correct and clear as you move from one position to the next.

2 This is where *petite* and *grande échappée* differ most. In *petite échappée*, open your legs directly to second position in the air. In *grande échappée*, keep your feet together in a tight fifth position as you jump up.

Petite *means small, and this jump is a low one.*

Grande *means big. This jump is higher.*

The need for strong muscles
Dancing the role of the frog Mr. Jeremy Fisher in *Tales of Beatrix Potter* involves a lot of jumping. Here, William Trevitt seems to hover in the air as he jumps from lily pad to lily pad. A jump like this needs strength and elasticity in the muscles and ligaments of the legs and feet. Careful preparation provides for good jumps. If your muscles are used properly from the beginning of your training, your dancing will look poised and fluent as you advance.

3 In *petite échappée*, land after opening your legs to second. For *grande échappée*, open your legs to second only at the moment of your return to the floor. Keep your *demi-plié* very even with the whole of each foot on the floor.

Hold your turnout.

Sissonne simple
This is a jump from two legs onto one. *Demi-plié* in fifth position and push off the floor using your heels, insteps, and toes. Bring your head up straight and use your arms to help you. Feel as if your whole body is gathered up into the air. Land on one leg, the other neatly in *cou de pied*.

4 Without releasing your muscles, push strongly off the floor. Fix second position in the air, keeping your legs taut and your toes pointed. Try to increase your turnout. Keep your arms flexible but properly placed – simple and low for *petite échappée*; higher and wider for *grande échappée*.

5 Land again in fifth position in a soft but steady and elastic *demi-plié*. Stretch your legs to finish. With more experience, you may do an *échappée* to fourth position, *croisé* or *effacé*. Your teacher may also ask you to finish on one leg instead of two.

Do not roll over onto your big or little toes.

Keep the whole of your foot on the floor.

Bigger jumps

WHEN your muscles have developed strength and resilience in simple jumps, you can attempt the larger jumps of *grand allegro*. These jumps are exciting, but also very demanding. You must be thoroughly prepared and completely warmed up before attempting them. In ballet, the way you enter a jump, hold it in the air, and complete it must all be artistic and precise. Enthusiasm, intelligence, and sensitivity will help you transform the merely physical and gymnastic into art.

As in all sissonnes, *make sure that your head is moving in harmony with your arms and body.*

Jumping balletically

There are many kinds of jumps. They can bounce, skim across the floor, or soar into the air. Each jump has its own look and feel, giving a variety of possibilities to choreographers. Here, Miyako Yoshida of The Birmingham Royal Ballet is performing a *grand jeté* in attitude from Ashton's ballet *La Fille mal Gardée.*

Sissonne fondue

This is a jump from the *sissonne* family. *Sissonnes* can be large or small, landing on one leg or closing quickly. They can be swift and neat, or they can soar into the air. You can even beat or turn them. *Sissonnes* start from two feet and have a flying quality whatever the speed, height, and direction. After landing in *sissonne fondue*, close your raised leg smoothly to fifth position. Your final *demi-plié* should be soft and melting.

Prepare carefully

It is important that the preparations that lead you into a jump are correct rhythmically and physically. Then you will get the proper impetus off the ground and a good shape in the air.

Ballonné

At first you will learn this jump *sur place*, or on the spot. Later you will learn to travel, flying forward, backward, or sideways, doing one *ballonné* after another. *Ballonné* should be rhythmical and staccato – like bouncing. It needs beautiful coordination and the positions of your arms and head must be exact.

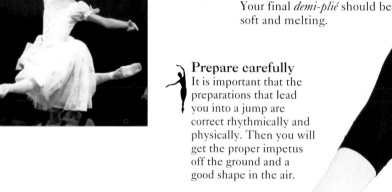

1 This is a *ballonné* to the side in second position. Start in fifth position with *épaulement croisé*.

2 *Demi-plié* as you slide your foot out, and push powerfully and energetically up off the floor.

3 Throw your leg strongly and cleanly to second position in the air, keeping a vertical line through your body.

Once in the air, stretch your legs, hold the shape, and then return safely to the ground.

On stage
Fiona Chadwick and Jonathan Cope, both performing a *grand jeté* in *La Bayadère*, show an exciting part of advanced *grand allegro*. *Grand allegro* can be developed in many ways in the progression from class to the stage.

Ballon
Appearing to hover at the high point of certain jumps is called *ballon*.

Pas de chat
This movement imitates the jump of a cat. (*Pas de chat* means "step of the cat.") There are several different forms of *pas de chat*, and they all need exact coordination of the body, arms, and legs. For this version, prepare your arms and then *demi-plié* in fifth position. Quickly lift your back foot to *cou de pied derrière*, then spring lightly upward and forward into the air, arms in front of you. At the end of the jump, close into a *demi-plié* in fifth position, with your arms and head completing the picture.

Bring this leg through quickly and lightly.

Keep your shoulders and thighs level, and fix the shape in the air.

Don't sit in your demi-pliés. Spring quickly into the air to show the position immediately.

Precise and sensitive footwork is essential for good elevation.

4 Land in a *demi-plié*, simultaneously closing your raised leg to *cou de pied devant*.

5 Spring quickly off the ground again to exactly the same position in the air.

6 Finish the second *ballonné* in *cou de pied derrière*. Be careful to land on balance.

On your toes

BALLERINAS FIRST danced on the tips of their toes at the beginning of the 19th century. It made them appear weightless and fragile, and this became an important and admired quality of ballet in the 1830s and 40s. Good pointework looks effortless and expressive, but it is actually the result of very hard work. You should not attempt to dance on pointe until your feet and legs are sufficiently strong. This will probably be when you are about eleven years old, and when you have already trained carefully for several years.

For relevé *in fifth position, keep your legs taut, turned out, and very close together.*

Tie your ribbons neatly – tight enough to support you, but loose enough to leave your ankle free to move.

Rosin is made from the sap of fir trees. It crumbles into a white powder if you step on it.

Preparing to dance

After tying your shoes, put the tips of your toes into the rosin box, one foot at a time. A little rosin on your shoes will help you avoid slipping on a wooden floor. It should not be necessary on a vinyl floor, which is usually less slippery.

Perfect positioning

It is a wonderful feeling when you dance on the tips of your toes. You feel light and delicate. But do not try to dance on pointe until your body, legs, and feet are strong enough to lift you up and carefully take you down again. Try to keep a vertical line through the center of your feet. It is especially important not to allow your feet to sickle, or tilt sideways over your big or little toes, when on pointe. Sickling can lead to permanent injury.

Make sure the drawstrings in your shoes are comfortably pulled up and tucked in.

Relevé

1 You will start to dance on pointe with simple exercises facing the barre to gain strength and stability. To do this *relevé*, start in first position.

2 Move smoothly into a *demi-plié*, keeping your heels firmly on the floor. Holding your turnout, push strongly up onto pointe. Roll through your feet carefully back into a *demi-plié*.

Echappé

1 *Demi-plié* in fifth position, then spring lightly onto pointe in second. Skim your toes along the floor to "escape" from the *demi-plié*.

2 Keeping lifted and light, close your legs simultaneously back to *demi-plié* in fifth position.

Keep your back straight and poised.

Keep your knees and insteps stretched and still, with your weight evenly balanced over both feet.

Glissade

This gliding movement is one of the steps you will learn when you have gained enough strength and confidence to dance on pointe in centre practice.

Your head will complete each shape and movement. Your gaze should be focused, yet free.

You can use many different arm positions in this pose.

Concentrate on your legs and feet, but also remember to think about your arms. Try to make each movement a complete picture in which your whole body is in harmony.

Always sew your own ribbons into your shoes so that you get the fit exactly right.

1 Start with a *demi-plié* in fifth position and stretch your leg forward with a sliding movement. Lift your arms slightly and look gracefully into your hands.

2 Transfer your weight forward onto your front pointe exactly at the spot reached by your toes. Close your back foot tightly behind to form fifth position on pointe.

Pointe shoes

The tips of pointe shoes are made of layers of satin, paper, and a coarse material called burlap, glued together. New shoes feel stiff and hard and have no left and right. It takes time and care to break them in and make them conform to your feet. You need to feel as if your shoes are a second skin. Then you will be able to "speak with your feet."

Advanced Pointework

Y OUR REGULAR CLASSES and exercises will give you the basic strength you need to progress in pointework. But physical ability alone is not enough. You need many different qualities, such as poise, flexibility, balance, and lightness. These all need to be developed in harmony. Don't overemphasize one and forget about the others. Although you need strength for dancing on pointe, remember that it is essentially very graceful and feminine.

Relevé croisé derrière

As you progress, your work will become more intricate and artistic. Finally you will be ready to move from the classroom to the stage.

Elite Syncopations

Here, Zoltan Solymosi and I are dancing in Kenneth MacMillan's ballet *Elite Syncopations*. The ballet is set to ragtime music by several composers, including Scott Joplin.

Perfect pointe

You must resist the temptation to rely on your shoes to hold you up on pointe. It will not only make your work look dull and heavy, but will wear your shoes out much faster. Use your muscles instead. Try to balance perfectly on the tip of your toe. Your foot should look so strong and poised that the audience believes you could stand on pointe without a shoe! I am dancing here in *Elite Syncopations*.

Pointework technique

Sometimes you will want to move smoothly, holding each movement so that it melts into the next. For this you must be able to lower slowly from the tips of your toes. At other times you will want to move quickly and your footwork must be staccato, neat, and exciting.

Relevé attitude croisée devant

The costumes for Elite Syncopations *were designed by Ian Spurling. MacMillan wanted this dance in the ballet to look chic, yet refined.*

Attitude *croisée derrière*

Let your head and arms complement the line of your legs. The complete picture should be balanced and graceful.

Make sure that your supporting knee is completely stretched at the top of the movement. Capture the shape.

While your legs are working hard, your body should maintain a relaxed quality.

Think about what you are doing
With each step you do, have a clear idea of the different effects you are trying to achieve.

Stretched knees, taut leg muscles, and strong feet and ankles all help with stability on pointe.

As you spring forward onto pointe, throw your working leg out in front of you to 45°.

Keep your back strong, especially as you lower into your demi-plié.

Pas ballonné

You can travel forward, backward, or sideways with this step, and you can use *épaulement croisé* or *effacé*. Travel as you *relevé* and then roll down through your supporting foot. You can change your *port de bras* to create different images of this step.

This ballonné *is traveling* effacé en avant.

Pas de deux

AT THE BEGINNING of the 19th century, the difference between the dancing styles of men and women became much more obvious. Women moved lightly and gracefully, and began to dance on the tips of their toes, while men emphasized strength and nobility in their movements. The men began to lift and support the women and sweep them up in the air. So began the wonderful world of *pas de deux*. A *pas de deux* is, above all, an exciting partnership between two dancers, physically, musically, and artistically. Everything you do depends on your rapport with your partner, and you can inspire each other to greater heights as you dance.

Enchaînement

There are rules for every shape and movement you make together. With practice, you will understand enough to link steps together in simple choreographed sequences. These are called *enchaînements*.

Learning together

In *pas de deux* it is important that partners match each other physically, with the girl slightly smaller and lighter than the boy, but strong enough to dance the required steps. You will first learn correct placement through supported adage, when you work together without lifting. Practice feeling both your own central line of balance and its relationship to your work with your partner.

Dance in harmony

You must try to keep each part of your own body dancing in harmony, while also coordinating your movements with your partner. You must both learn to breathe and balance together and feel each other's rhythm. Boys must be sensitive to the movement of a girl when supporting, holding, or lifting her, so she can keep her balance.

The movement of your head is very important. It should move correctly and easily to any position.

The boy needs to support the girl confidently, but not be tense or rigid.

You must listen and respond to the music together.

The girl should not change her position until each particular movement is completed.

1 To work on and perform this *enchaînement*, prepare together to *tendu croisé derrière* with your arms in second position. Look out to the audience.

2 Let your heads lead the movement into a small waltz step. Make sure you are moving together both physically and musically, and that the balance of movement between you is artistic.

3 Now both change direction. The girl steps forward to first arabesque on pointe. The boy must be ready to judge how far away he must stand for the girl to keep her balance. He stands behind her with the palms of his hands placed firmly on the sides of her waist with his first finger and thumb encircling it.

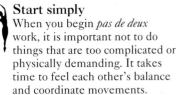

Start simply
When you begin *pas de deux* work, it is important not to do things that are too complicated or physically demanding. It takes time to feel each other's balance and coordinate movements.

Practice is important
Lifts require precise timing and coordination from both partners. I always practice with my partner, in this case Zoltan Solymosi, until we both know exactly what the other is going to do. Then we can feel, adjust, and prepare for a performance. I always remember that a great deal depends on how I start and finish each movement. This lift is from a *pas de deux* in the ballet *Swan Lake*.

Concentrate on complementing each other in line and movement.

4 Using his hands, the boy brings the girl's body upright as she closes her raised leg to fifth position. When he feels she is balanced, he lets go of her waist and lifts his arms to match hers. Make a clear picture together, then repeat the *enchaînement* on the other side.

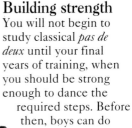

Building strength
You will not begin to study classical *pas de deux* until your final years of training, when you should be strong enough to dance the required steps. Before then, boys can do special exercises to build up their strength. They must only be done under careful supervision.

Lifting carefully
Zoltan has to concentrate hard throughout this lift. He has to make it look easy, and I obviously help him as much as I can by pushing off well from a good *demi-plié*. To avoid damaging his back, he must hold it firmly when lifting, and keep his weight centered through his body.

Even during difficult lifts, the man must always think about the aesthetic look of his position while also trying to portray the character of his role in the ballet.

Folk and character dancing

EVERY CULTURE has its own own collection of dances that are performed on formal and informal occasions. These dances, known as folk dances, may be taught in school, but many young people learn them from their elders, as a ritual of growing up. They express all kinds of feelings and moods: from happy to sad, from exuberant to reflective. When danced in towns and villages, they may have rough edges, but they are full of spirit and tradition. Choreographers like to introduce folk dances into their ballets to add color and movement, and to evoke the spirit of a particular nation or people. This stylized folk dancing is called character dancing.

Sabotière
This French dance was specially choreographed by the famous Russian ballet master Nicolai Legat. It tells the story of a girl and a boy meeting, dancing together, and finally stealing a kiss!

Coppélia
This is Sadler's Wells Royal Ballet (now The Birmingham Royal Ballet) performing *Coppélia*. In this ballet, there are several character dances based on folk dances. They contain some of the steps of the original dances, but are modified and embellished to fit in with the style of the ballet. This dance from Act I is based on a Polish mazurka.

Part of ballet
Whether or not you study character dancing as part of your training, by the time you perform many classical ballets, you will have learned many modified folk dances. You may be dancing in this Russian style just before performing a beautiful *pas de deux*!

These costumes for Sabotière are freely based on traditional designs from Brittany in France.

Many of the steps involve swinging your partner around.

Square dancing

This is a traditional form of dance found in the United States. It has developed from the country dances, round dances, square dances, and quadrilles of Europe. Traditionally, square dancing is led by a "caller" who chooses the steps and leads the dancers through them by singing, or "calling," instructions while the music is played.

The port de bras and footwork •have many balletic qualities.

Scottish dancing

There are two forms of Scottish dancing: highland and country. Highland dancing is an ancient form, originally performed only by men. Some dances, such as the *Gillie Chalium*, begin slowly, but end exuberantly, matching the emotional feeling created by the traditional bagpipe music. Country dancing is used in the ballroom, and is not considered folk dancing.

Your dancing must be strong, but light and athletic.

Shoes for character-dancing classes are a lighter version of normal leather lace-up or strap shoes, but with special non-slip soles and heels.

The costumes are embroidered with traditional Celtic designs.

Irish dancing

The special quality of Irish dancing comes from the contrast between the controlled elegance of the body and magical footwork. Although mostly based on simple steps, once warmed up, dancers can elaborate in extraordinary ways. This is one of the intricate steps of a double jig, based on syncopation and complex rhythms. The way you move across the floor and the rhythms you use are important and can be very exciting.

In some dancing, you may wear hard tapping shoes like these, but soft shoes are best for intricate footwork.

Mime and makeup

EVER SINCE Ancient Greek times, mime has been used in the theater as a way of expressing ideas, feelings, and plots with gestures rather than words. During its development, a number of gestures took on particular meanings. Under the influence of early dancing masters, some of these gestures became a part of ballet choreography. This kind of mime is not used so much in new ballets, but you will need to know a little about it to understand and perform in classic ballets such as *Giselle*, *Swan Lake*, and *The Sleeping Beauty*. It is a small, but important part of the ballet tradition, so learn and enjoy it.

A serious art
Take your mimes seriously. Do not exaggerate your movements or be flippant.

Beg or beseech
Stand or kneel with your hands clasped in front of you. Then bring your hands close to you and bow your head.

Baby
You usually start a gesture with your arms in a natural first or second position. Slowly, with a flowing movement, move your arms into the specific gesture. For this mime, bring your arms together as if you are gently cradling a baby.

Sleep for men
Put your hands together against your cheek and rest your head gently on them.

Your gestures should be beautiful and harmonious, as well as expressive.

Mime with feeling
When performing a gesture, draw your audience into the story with the power of your mime.

Sleep for women
Place your arms as if you are resting on a table and close your eyes. When miming, aim for simplicity, clarity, and directness.

46

Kill

Pretend to take a dagger from its scabbard, raise it up into the air, and plunge it into your heart.

Although in mime you use your whole body expressively, the precise meaning is conveyed especially by your arms and hands.

Fright

This is the moment in *Swan Lake* (Act II) when, as the beautiful and tragic Princess Odette, I am startled by the sudden appearance of Prince Siegfried at the lakeside. Odette is frightened and wants to hide.

Makeup

Theaters today have powerful lights that are used creatively and dramatically. Makeup is therefore essential for dancers, to prevent washed out or shiny appearances. It is part of a dancer's art to be able to put on makeup for different circumstances and characters.

1 Choose a base color for your face that is suitable for your character. Apply the makeup with a damp sponge. Blend it into your neck so that it does not look like a mask.

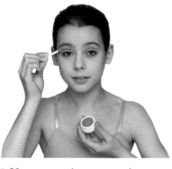

2 Use eye makeup to make your eyes stand out from a distance. Ask a friend to tell you what it looks like. The effect is often quite different from a distance.

3 Choose your lip color according to the color of the lights. For example, if the lights are very blue, red lipstick will look black. Pink would be better.

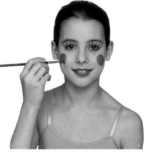

4 To make yourself up as a doll, like the famous one in Fokine's *Petrushka*, draw five or six "lashes" above your eyes with a black pencil.

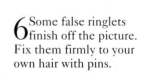

5 Then paint round red spots on your cheeks. Draw circles with a steady hand and fill them in.

6 Some false ringlets finish off the picture. Fix them firmly to your own hair with pins.

Wash immediately Water-based makeup allows you to wash it all off with soap and warm water.

Preparing for a performance

SCENERY and costumes have traditionally been an essential part of ballet. It is difficult to imagine *Les Sylphides* without the soft, dreamlike white dresses and the mysterious woodland glade, or *Petrushka* without the fairground. So when you put on your own performance, remember that the design of the ballet is as important as its music in creating its mood. From Leonardo da Vinci in the 16th century to Picasso in this century, great artists have influenced ballet productions and costume designs, changing styles dramatically from the heavy bejeweled dresses of the early court days, to the tutus of the 19th century, to the body-clinging tights of today. Designers are now able to draw on many styles to create dynamic new productions.

A crown for a queen can be made from cardboard painted gold.

A fairy's wings can be made of wire bent to shape and covered with gauze.

Costume

A ballet costume usually has to be worn for many performances so it must be strong, comfortable, and safe. Take great care when you are trying on a costume. Make sure it fits properly and that it does not restrict your movements. If you can, put it to the test in a dress rehearsal.

Ask a friend to help you practice putting your headdress on.

Hair and headdress

Your hair, headdress, and makeup will make all the difference in how you look and also how you dance. Choose something simple to suit the character you are playing. Make sure you can secure wigs or headdresses firmly. If you are confident that your appearance is right, you will be able to put all your thoughts and energy into your dancing.

The wardrobe mistress makes, alters, and cares for a school's costumes.

Improvise if you don't have something you need. These boots are laced with string.

Wardrobe

Many schools have a wardrobe department. It is an exciting place full of lycra, velvet, silk, chiffon, and perhaps even some suede and fake fur. All this can be made up into costumes to fit the dancers. Extra dye color, beads, braid, and ribbons can be used to change a costume dramatically for different productions.

Pieces of the material to be used are attached to the design.

This scenery is being painted for an English National Ballet production of Swan Lake.

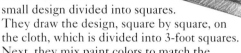

Painting scenery

Some scenes have to be painted on huge pieces of cloth. The cloth is nailed onto a frame and primed with white primer. The artists work from a small design divided into squares. They draw the design, square by square, on the cloth, which is divided into 3-foot squares. Next, they mix paint colors to match the colors of the design. Then they "lay in" the cloth using brushes anywhere from 3 to 6 inches wide. When the cloth is dry, the finishing touches are done from a small paint pallette.

Costume design

These costume designs are for the 1993 production of the 19th-century ballet *Le Corsaire* by the Memphis Concert Ballet. The notes down the side are from the artist and describe the costumes in detail. The designs are evocative and practical – two essential elements of good costume design.

Set design

The French painter and designer Christian Bérard did this set design for *Symphonie Fantastique* in 1936.

The Sleeping Princess

This design was by Bakst for the Diaghilev production of *The Sleeping Princess* in 1921. It shows an idea for the arrival of Prince Charming. Diaghilev was a major personality in the art world and formed the Ballet Russe.

The performance

O N THE DAY of a performance, after weeks of hard work, everyone is busy putting the finishing touches on a new ballet. Musicians, designers, stage staff, set builders, and dressmakers all have very important and specific roles to play. If you are in a performance, make sure you are fully prepared. No one wants any last-minute problems or jitters.

On stage

Footlights

Downstage left	Downstage right

Wings — Wings

Upstage left	Upstage right

Back cloth

Stage directions have names so that dancers can follow a choreographer's instructions. When you choreograph a ballet, find out the shape and size of the stage and arrange your dancers in a logical and balanced way. Rehearse on stage to get used to the space. You can use tape to mark particular places.

A ballet to perform

Here is a suggestion for a ballet, or you can make up your own story.

The audience needs to see her despair.

Perform this with a dreamlike quality.

Act I

Scene 1 A royal court
In a wonderful and magical land, there rules a king and queen. The prince, their son and heir, is betrothed to a lovely princess.

But the prince is in love with a poor serving maid and she with him. She realizes the hopelessness of their situation and decides to leave the castle.

The day of the prince's marriage is set, but the sad prince can think only of the serving maid. Her spirit is always with him.

The first shy moment.

Act II

Scene 1   A forest clearing
After many months of struggle and adventure, the prince and his friend stumble into a clearing in the forest. They see the serving maid sitting alone, wrapped in her own thoughts. The prince calls softly to her. She looks up and, in that moment, they realize that their lives are eternally bound together.

They dance a pas de deux, nervous and hesitant at first, becoming more passionate as they go on. The prince persuades the maid to return home to his kingdom with him.

Scene 2   The castle gardens
Guided by the Fairy of Happiness, the queen meets the maid in the castle garden. She discovers the truth about the couple's love. She is entranced by the girl and realizes she should allow her son to marry the serving maid.

Joining the stars
You may be lucky enough to dance on stage with a professional ballet company. If you ever get this chance, you will enter a magic world full of color and emotion, and the excitement will be unforgettable. These children are dancing with Georgette Farias of the Stuttgart Ballet in *The Sleeping Beauty*.

The final curtain
During the applause at the end of a performance, a ballerina often receives a gift of flowers. Then, as she makes her final graceful curtsies, the curtain falls, and the performance is over.

Charmaine Hunter of the Dance Theatre of Harlem receives flowers and applause at the end of a performance of The Firebird.

This is a moment when you could use your knowledge of mime.

The fairy looks into the distance to "say" that it will be a hard and difficult journey.

Scene 2   A forest clearing
As the maid travels away from the castle, she meets the Fairy of Happiness and begs for help. The fairy promises to try to bring the couple together, but tells the maid she must be patient.

Scene 3   The prince's rooms
The fairy appears to the prince in a dream. She tells him that he must go on a journey if he wants to find happiness.

The prince tells his friend about his dream. The friend advises him to follow the fairy's instructions and agrees to go with him on the journey. As they run off stage, the curtain falls on Act I.

Later, the prince's friend, who has always secretly loved the princess, finally declares his love for her. With a soft glance, the princess realizes she has found the man she always sought. They dance together, happy to have found each other.

Scene 3   The royal court
There is a double wedding. The two couples have the blessing of the king and queen and everyone enjoys the splendor and gaiety of the celebrations.

My life as a ballet dancer

BEING A PRINCIPAL ballerina is a wonderful experience and I enjoy all the challenges it presents. I perform all over the world, working with male principals from other countries to portray many different styles of *pas de deux*, and I have seen the varied reactions that ballets receive in different cultures. I have been fortunate to perform in many classic ballets, but working on ballets with new choreographers and adapting to their individual styles is something I always look forward to. I love a dancer's life, but it is not all so interesting and exciting. I must constantly practice, striving for perfection, and I always have to be in control for every performance I give.

Shoes are very personal because every dancer has different feet. I use both ribbons and elastic to keep my shoes secure.

Ballet shoes

As each ballet contains a number of different movements, I need more than one pair of ballet shoes. In scenes containing lots of jumping, I wear soft pointe shoes so that they do not make a noise when I land. For technical pointe work, such as turning and balancing, I wear slightly harder shoes to give my feet more support. I try to rehearse steps in the same type of shoes I will use on stage.

I often prepare three or four pairs of ballet shoes for one performance.

Keeping my hair neat

It is important for me to keep my hair up and out of the way, so that it does not distract me when I am rehearsing. I must also be careful to keep my hair out of my partner's eyes.

Tutus

I only wear a tutu when performing classical ballets. I rehearse these ballets in a practice tutu so that my partner and I can get used to it.

Warming up

Warming up is essential before any rehearsal, because it is easy to strain cold muscles. I do lots of slow, repetitive stretching exercises for all the different muscle groups. Between rehearsals I wear legwarmers or a tracksuit to keep my muscles warm.

I wear a headdress to complement my costume. It has jewels that catch the light as I move. I have to make sure it is securely pinned to my hair before a performance.

Performing in *Swan Lake*

One of the most challenging classical ballets in which I have performed is *Swan Lake*. One minute I am the soft, white swan Odette, and the next I am the devious, black swan Odile. *Swan Lake* contains lots of difficult steps, and I need sustained confidence and stamina to perform it. At the same time it is very exhilarating.

The detail on my tutu is light and subtle, but sufficient to portray the character I am playing. The white feathers represent the white swan Odette.

Rehearsing

I might have three or four rehearsals in a day for different ballets. When rehearsing my solos, I have to repeat some steps again and again until they are perfect. My teacher guides me to improve some of the harder movements. Some steps can require several weeks of practice before I am happy with them.

Hard work

My partner and I must trust each other because a lot of the *pas de deux* moves in *Swan Lake*, and other ballets, are difficult. They can be dangerous if performed half-heartedly. We therefore have to prepare the *pas de deux* movements carefully.

Other dance forms

BALLET IS only one of many dance forms ranging from tap to ballroom. Contemporary, or modern, dance is a freer form than classical ballet, as are many of the forms associated with jazz, the theater, and popular music. Some are first and foremost social activities that anyone can enjoy, regardless of physique or age. But if you want to dance seriously, you will need to take lessons. As you study any of the various forms, you will discover that each has its own history, experts, and traditions.

Tap shoes have toe and heel taps fitted to make special sounds on the floor.

Jazz dance
This style of dancing is a North American tradition that developed from a mixture of African and European dances. Today it is used extensively in musicals, and is often referred to as show, or commercial, dance.

Jazz dance is lively and fun and full of color and rhythm.

Contemporary dance
What we call contemporary dance is now nearly 100 years old. It started with the American "modern dancers" Isadora Duncan and Loïe Fuller. They devised what they felt was a freer and more natural form of expressive dance. Martha Graham and Merce Cunningham, among others, later developed specific traditions of contemporary dance, each with its own technique, style, and training.

Cats
Gillian Lynne was a dancer with the company then called Sadler's Wells Ballet before she turned to choreography. For *Cats*, she devised slow stretching movements and also included some jazz and tap. For shows like this, a classical ballet training is invaluable.

Use your whole body to tap dance, not just your feet and ankles.

Tap dancing

Like jazz, tap is an American art that has its roots in slavery. The African slaves mixed their traditional dances with the jigs and clog dances of the European Americans. So was born a new tapping, swinging style of dance that is performed throughout the world.

You will need to move quickly and rhythmically to tap dance. It is important that you understand where your center of balance is.

Starlight Express

Modern musicals can make all kinds of demands on dancers. *Starlight Express*, choreographed by Arlene Phillips, is famous for the dancers' daredevil acrobatics and circus stunts – all on roller skates!

Gesture in contemporary dance is emotionally evocative.

42nd Street

The overture ends and the curtain rises just enough for the audience to see 30 pairs of tapping feet! The choreographer of *42nd Street*, Gower Champion, used bold theatrical effects like this to pay homage to the 1930s style of dancers such as Fred Astaire.

In contemporary dance, you can be inventive with the use of movements on the floor.

The movements in contemporary dance are expressive and supple.

Contemporary dancers often dance barefoot.

Choreography

A CHOREOGRAPHER'S role in ballet is like that of a composer's in music, or an artist's in painting. But unlike a composer or a painter, the choreographer's materials are living people. The choreographer decides on the theme of the ballet, its music, and its story, and creates steps for the dancers to perform. Often a ballet is created for specific dancers with steps that show off the dancers' particular talents. Great choreographers such as Petipa, Balanchine, and Ashton all developed their own styles, and the companies of dancers with whom they worked became especially expert and experienced in performing their works.

Bintley
After deciding on the story for a ballet, a choreographer will imagine the movements and try them out with dancers. Here, David Bintley is showing dancers what he wants for his ballet *The Swan of Tuonela*. Bintley is one of today's most exciting choreographers. His work is sensitive and wide-ranging, covering many styles and themes.

"Still Life" at the Penguin Café
One of David Bintley's ballets is *"Still Life" at the Penguin Café*. He set it to fascinating and unusual music by Simon Jeffes. It is a thought-provoking ballet, both touching and funny. Through dance, Bintley makes the audience think about the consequences of allowing animals to become extinct.

Bintley's choreography conjures up a zebra, performed by Phillip Broomhead, wandering in the whispering grasses of the African savannah.

The monkey's very essence is captured by movements created for Stephen Jefferies.

Benesh notation

Until this century, there was no secure way of recording the steps of ballet. Ballets were passed on by dancers and choreographers through memory. Because of this, many early ballets have been lost. During this century, a number of different ways of notating dance have been developed. This is called choreology. One of the most popular methods is Benesh notation. It is named after Rudolf and Joan Benesh, who invented it in the late 1940s. Benesh notation is written on a five line staff, like a music staff. It is placed below the music staff so that both the music and the movement can be read together.

Benesh notation for arabesque

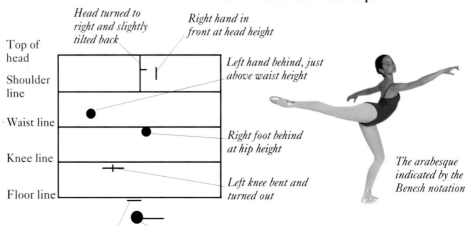

Head turned to right and slightly tilted back

Right hand in front at head height

Top of head

Shoulder line

Left hand behind, just above waist height

Waist line

Knee line

Right foot behind at hip height

Floor line

Left knee bent and turned out

Dancer is standing on flat of left foot.

Dancer is facing stage left.

The arabesque indicated by the Benesh notation

Balanchine

George Balanchine (1904-1983) created more than 100 ballets, including *Serenade, Apollo, The Four Temperaments,* and *Symphony in C.* Born and trained in Russia, he moved to New York in 1933, after working in Europe. He devised a new classic style, part Russian, and part American. His ballets are often abstract in theme and without a plot. They are both athletic and graceful, complex and clear. Balanchine is shown here working closely with his dancers.

Members of the Kirov Ballet in Apollo. *Apollo's muses form a clean but complex pattern as they urge him toward beauty.*

Keeping ballet alive

Ballets choreographed many years ago are still performed today by different companies all over the world. Obviously, the choreographer of a ballet cannot always be there to show dancers what to do. Although ballets can now be recorded on film or by notation, full knowledge of how to perform them can only be handed on from one dancer to another. The tradition of teaching is therefore a vital link between the past and the future.

Patricia Neary rehearsing Apollo *with the Kirov Ballet*

Apollo

In 1928, *Apollo* marked the arrival of Balanchine as a great choreographer. He brought back to ballet a purity of line and gesture that had long been lost. This is one of the 12 ballets that Balanchine choreographed to Stravinsky's music. Balanchine maintained that his Apollo was not the traditional perfect god, but "a wild half-human youth who acquires nobility through art."

Les Sylphides

It now seems that this is the classic Romantic *ballet blanc*, or white ballet, steeped in feminine beauty and lovely, gauzy costumes. Yet it was not created in the 1840s, as were most of the Romantic ballets, but rather in 1908, by Michael Fokine in Russia. It was originally called *Chopiniana*, and still is in Russia, because it is danced to music by Chopin. Although it has no plot, the dancers suggest a moonlit romance. This eight-bar phrase in Benesh notation is from the prelude solo of Fokine's ballet, leading up to the quiet moment shown in the picture.

Natalia Makarova as a guest dancer with The Royal Ballet in Les Sylphides

Going to the ballet

ONE OF THE EXCITING things about watching ballet is the variety of different styles. You can enter the mysterious world of heroes and sylphs in the Romantic ballets, or see the grandeur and jewellike splendor of Petipa's work. Then there are the exotic ballets of the Diaghilev era, with brilliant dancers, musicians, and designers, or the clear beauty of Balanchine. You can absorb the culture, poetry, and humor of Ashton, or the drama and psychological power of MacMillan. Or you may prefer modern ballets, which experiment with forms and feelings. When you buy your ticket for a ballet, make sure you will be able to see the stage clearly. If you have a seat high up in the theater, you will be able to see all the floor patterns the dancers are making, as well as their entrances and exits. Here are some ballets you can watch for.

The Australian Ballet

Suite en blanc
This ballet without a story was choreographed by Lifar to music by Lalo and was first performed in Paris in 1943. It involves a large company. The girls wear white tutus and the men wear white shirts. The stage is divided into two tiers and the possibilities of movement are fully exploited.

The Bavarian Ballet

Les Noces (The Wedding)
This ballet is a remarkable piece of dance theater. It was first performed in 1923 and was very unlike a conventional ballet. *Les Noces* represents a Russian peasant wedding with great vigor, power, and earthiness. Originally choreographed by Bronislava Nijinska with music and words by Stravinsky, the version shown here is choreographed by Jiri Kylian.

The Frankfurt Ballet

Petrushka
Representing a crowded fairground, Fokine's *Petrushka* captures all the movement and excitement of the fair. In one booth, a magician makes three dolls dance. At dusk, in the back of their booth, the dolls come alive.

The Royal Ballet

Steptext
This ballet is only 17 minutes long. It is choreographed by William Forsythe, one of the most exciting choreographers in the world today. His works push both the language of dance and the dancers themselves to new extremes.

Touchbase
This modern ballet is choreographed by Merce Cunningham, a leading figure in experimental dance. His work aims to show human movement in all its variety.

Rambert Dance Company

Romeo and Juliet

Many choreographers, including Sir Frederick Ashton and Sir Kenneth MacMillan, have choreographed a version of this ballet based on Shakespeare's play. The music most often used today is that by Sergei Prokoviev.

The Dance Theatre of Harlem

Margot Fonteyn and Rudolf Nureyev were the first stars of MacMillan's ballet.

The program
Try to read the program before the performance begins. Even if the ballet does not have a story, there will be lots of information about the music, the dancers, and the choreographers. The more you know about what you are watching, the more you will enjoy it.

The Four Temperaments

This ballet by Balanchine has no plot. It is based on the medieval idea that a human being contains four humors: the melancholic (gloomy), the sanguine (cheerful), the phlegmatic (unexcitable), and the choleric (angry). Between the ballet's opening theme and finale, each humor has its own variation.

The Sleeping Beauty

This is a classic full-length fairy tale ballet, with court scenes, good and bad fairies, a beautiful princess, and a brave, handsome prince. It was originally choreographed by Marius Petipa in 1890, but there have been many versions since. *The Sleeping Beauty* is the supreme classical ballet. It represents the ultimate challenge for a classical ballerina.

The Royal Ballet

Moscow Classical Ballet

A Month in the Country

Sir Frederick Ashton choreographed this ballet in 1976. It is based on a play by Ivan Turgenev. Ashton compressed humor, passion, drama, character, and the atmosphere of a lazy summer vacation all into one act.

Useful addresses

Studying dancing can be very enjoyable whether you want to dance as a hobby or a career. But if you want to go to a professional school, you will probably have to audition. Instructors look for a particular type of body shape and a certain ability to turn out, as well as enthusiasm and motivation. If you are accepted, you will have to be extremely dedicated. Below are the addresses of a few well known companies with affiliated schools that you may want to write to. However, there are many more companies and schools throughout the US. Your local library should be able to help you find some in your area, where you can get started right away!

A ballet class at the Royal Ballet School

American Ballet Theatre
890 Broadway
New York, NY 10003
(212) 477-3030

The Joffrey Ballet
130 West 56th Street
New York, NY 10019
(212) 265-7300

Stephen Jefferies in "Still Life" *at the Penguin Café for The Royal Ballet*

Dance Theatre of Harlem
247 West 30th Street
New York, NY 10001
(212) 967-3470

New York City Ballet
New York State Theater
20 Lincoln Center Plaza
New York, NY 10023
(212) 870-5656

Merce Cunningham Dance Company
55 Bethune Street
New York, NY 10014
(212) 255-8240

Alvin Ailey American Dance Theater
211 West 61st Street
3rd Floor
New York, NY 10023
(212) 767-0590

Martha Graham Dance Company
316 East 63rd Street
New York, NY 10021
(212) 832-9166

Ballet Chicago
222 South Riverside Plaza
Suite 865
Chicago, IL 60606
(312) 993-7575

Ballet Florida
500 Fern Street
West Palm Beach, FL 33401
(407) 659-1212

Miami City Ballet
905 Lincoln Road
Miami Beach, FL 33139
(305) 532-4880

Colorado Ballet
1278 Lincoln
Denver, CO 80203
(303) 837-8888

Boston Ballet
19 Clarendon Street
Boston, MA 02116
(617) 695-6950

Dayton Ballet
140 North Main Street
Dayton, OH 45402
(513) 449-5060

Milwaukee Ballet
504 West National Avenue
Milwaukee, WI 53204
(414) 643-7677

Pacific Northwest Ballet
301 Mercer Street
Seattle, WA 98109
(206) 441-9411

The Pennsylvania Ballet
1101 South Broad Street
Philadelphia, PA 19147
(215) 551-7000

Pittsburgh Ballet Theatre
2900 Liberty Avenue
Pittsburgh, PA 15201
(412) 281-6727

San Francisco Ballet
455 Franklin Street
San Francisco, CA 94102
(415) 861-5600

The Washington Ballet
3515 Wisconsin Avenue N.W.
Washington, D.C. 20016
(202) 362-3606

Houston Ballet
1921 West Bell
Houston, TX 77019
(713) 523-6300

Details of a selection of ballets

Apollo (1928)
Music: Stravinsky
Choreography: Balanchine
Follows Apollo from his birth, his education, and his final ascent of Mount Parnassus.

L'Après-midi d'un faune (1912)
Music: Debussy
Choreography: Nijinsky
A faun, playing on his flute one summer afternoon, falls in love with a nymph.

La Bayadère (1877)
Music: Minkus
Choreography: M. Petipa
Tells of a love triangle between the bayadère Nikya, Solor, and Gamzatti.

Cinderella
Music: Prokofiev
Choreography: versions by Ashton and others
Based on Perrault's famous fairy tale about the fate of Cinderella and Prince Charming despite interference from the two ugly sisters.

Coppélia (1870)
Music: Delibes
Choreography: Saint-Léon
Combines the romance between Swanilda and Franz with the story of the doll-maker Coppelius, who tries to create a doll with a soul, called Coppélia.

Le Corsaire (1856)
Music: Adam and others
Choreography: Mazilier
Based on Lord Byron's poem The Corsair about a Greek girl sold into slavery.

The Dream (1964)
Music: Mendelssohn
Choreography: Ashton
Roughly following the plot of Shakespeare's A Midsummer Night's Dream, it centers around an argument between Titania and Oberon over a mysterious Indian boy and the loves of Helena.

Elite Syncopations (1974)
Music: S. Joplin and others
Choreography: MacMillan
A ragtime ballet set in a dance hall.

The Firebird (1910)
Music: Stravinsky
Choreography: Fokine
Based on various Russian fairy tales, it tells of Prince Ivan who captures the Firebird.

Giselle (1841)
Music: Adam
Choreography: Coralli and Perrot
Follows the romance between a peasant girl, Giselle, and Albrecht, a Count.

Medea (1950)
Music: Bartók
Choreography: Cullberg
Ballet of love and revenge, based on an Ancient Greek legend.

A Month in the Country (1976)
Music: Chopin
Choreography: Ashton
Based on a play by Turgenev about the love-triangle between Natalia Petrovna, her ward Vera, and a tutor, Beliaev.

Les Noces (1923)
Music: Stravinsky
Choreography: Nijinska
Based on a Russian wedding ritual.

The Nutcracker (1892)
Music: Tchaikovsky
Choreography: Ivanov
Tells the story of Klara, who is given a nutcracker for Christmas. At night, all her gifts come to life.

Petrushka (1911)
Music: Stravinsky
Choreography: Fokine
The owner of a puppet theater has three puppets, Petrushka, the Ballerina, and the Moor, who come to life.

The Prince of the Pagodas (1957)
Music: Britten
Choreography: Cranko
A fairy-tale ballet about the Emperor of the Middle Kingdom and his two daughters.

Romeo and Juliet
Music: Prokofiev
Choreography: versions by Ashton, MacMillan, and others
Follows Shakespeare's tragedy of social conflict.

The Sleeping Beauty (1890)
Music: Tchaikovsky
Choreography: Petipa
Based on Perrault's famous fairy tale.

Solitaire (1956)
Music: M. Arnold
Choreography: MacMillan
Concerns a girl who repeatedly tries to join in the activities of her friends, but always finds herself left alone.

Steptext (1984)
Music: Bach
Choreography: Forsythe
Ballet that pushes both the art form and dancers to new extremes.

"Still Life" at the Penguin Café (1988)
Music: Jeffes
Choreography: Bintley
Ballet that makes us think about the environment.

Swan Lake (1895)
Music: Tchaikovsky
Choreography: Petipa/Ivanov
The story of Princess Odette, who is turned into a swan.

Les Sylphides (1907)
Music: Chopin
Choreography: Fokine
A young man dances with the spirits of young women.

Tales of Beatrix Potter (1971)
Music: Lanchbery
Choreography: Ashton
A ballet in which the best loved of Beatrix Potter's characters are portrayed.

Theme and Variations (1947)
Music: Tchaikovsky
Choreography: Balanchine
A plotless ballet set to the final movement of Tchaikovsky's Suite No. 3 in G major.

Touchbase (1992)
Music: Pugilese
Choreography: Cunningham
Ballet that looks at human movement in all its variety.

Fiona Chadwick and Jonathan Cope in La Bayadère

Glossary

You will find many of the words on these pages useful during your ballet classes.

A

Adage Derived from the musical term *adagio*, meaning at ease or leisure. Slow and graceful movements.

Air, en l' In the air. When the working leg is in the air.

Allegro Taken from the Italian musical term meaning brisk and lively. Quick movements.

Allongé Extended or outstretched.

Arabesque A pose on one leg with the other leg extended behind and the body forming a graceful curve.

Arrière, en Backward. When a step is performed backward, away from the audience.

Assemblé Assembled. A jump in which the legs are brought together in the air before landing in fifth position.

Attitude A pose on one leg with the other leg lifted either backward or forward and bent at the knee.

Avant, en Forward. When a step is performed forward, toward the audience.

B

Ballet blanc White ballet. Any ballet in which the ballerinas wear traditional long white dresses, as designed for Marie Taglioni to wear in *La Sylphide* in 1830.

Ballet d'action A ballet with a story.

Ballon Bounce. The elastic quality of a jump.

Ballonné A bouncing jump in which the dancer lands on one leg in *demi-plié* with the working foot *sur le cou de pied*.

Barre The hand rail used by dancers to help them balance while exercising.

Barrework Initial exercises of daily classroom work, performed at the barre.

Battement Beating. A beating action of the working leg when extended or bent. There are many types of battement, small and large.

Battement frappé A strong striking movement of the working leg away from *cou de pied* to a low extended position in front, to the side, or behind.

Battement tendu A movement in which the working leg is stretched along the floor to a fully extended position.

Battement tendu jeté A movement in which the working leg is "thrown" into the air at a low height.

Batterie Beating. Movements in which the legs beat against each other in the air. There are many different types.

Bras Arm.

C

Center of balance An imaginary line through your body on which you are evenly balanced in a particular pose.

Centre practice Exercises performed in the center of the room, away from the barre.

Character dancing A style of dancing derived from national, traditional, or folk dances.

Changement de pieds Changing feet. A small or large jump in which the feet change position in the air.

Choreographer The person who composes or invents a ballet or dance, and arranges the steps.

Choreography The actual steps and patterns of a ballet or dance.

Choreology The recording of ballet in notation form.

Classical ballet The traditional ballet technique. **Also:** A ballet from the second half of the 19th century that displays the classical technique.

Contemporary dancing A modern style of dancing that is freer than classical ballet.

Corps de ballet A group of dancers who perform in support of soloists and leading dancers.

Cou de pied Neck of the foot. A position of the working foot on or around the ankle of the supporting leg.

Croisé Crossed. A position in which the body is turned slightly and the line of the legs is crossed to the audience.

D

Dedans, en Inward. When a movement, step, or turn of the body is toward the supporting leg.

Dégagé Disengaged. When the foot is pointed in an open position with a fully arched instep.

Dehors, en Outward. When a movement, step, or turn of the body is away from the supporting leg.

Demi-plié Half-bend. A position in which the knees are half bent.

Demi-pointes Half-points. When a dancer stands on the ball of their feet.

Derrière Behind. When a movement, step, or placement of an arm or leg is done behind the body.

Dessous Under. When the working foot passes behind the supporting foot.

Dessus Over. When the working foot passes in front of the supporting foot.

Devant In front. When a movement, step, or placement of an arm or leg is done in front of the body.

Développé Developed. An unfolding movement of the working leg into an open position in the air.

Divertissement Diversion, enjoyment. Short dances inserted into a classic ballet to display the talents of individuals or groups of dancers.

E

Ecarté Separated or thrown wide apart. A basic pose in which a dancer's leg is in second position, but the whole body is placed diagonally to the audience.

Echappée Escaped. A movement of both legs simultaneously into an open position, performed on the floor or in the air.

Effacé A position in which the body is turned slightly, and the line of the legs is open to the audience.

Elévation Height. The height achieved in any jumping movement.

Enchaînement Linking. A number of steps linked together.

Épaulement Shouldered. A particular and artistic placement of the shoulders, head, and body as a dancer turns a little toward or away from the audience.

F

Face, en Facing. When a dancer faces straight out to the audience.

Fermé Closed. When the feet are in a closed position.

Folk dancing A type of dancing that has developed through the traditions of a culture, and been passed down from generation to generation.

Fondu Melting. A smooth melting movement.

Frappé Struck. As, for example, in *battement frappé*.

G

Grand Large. As, for example, in *grand allegro*.

Glissade A gliding step that can be either jumped or taken smoothly up onto pointe.

Grand allegro The larger jumps and traveling steps of *allegro*.

Grand battement A quick and energetic "throw" of the leg into the air.

Grande échappée A version of the jump *échappée sautée*, in which the legs are opened only at the moment of the return to the floor.

Grand jeté A big jump from one leg to the other, with legs outstretched in the air.

Grand plié A position in which the legs are fully bent.

J

Jambe Leg.

Jazz dancing A style of dancing that developed in North America, from a mixture of African and European folk dances.

Jeté Thrown. As, for example, in *battement jeté*.

M

Modern ballet A type of ballet from this century.

N

Notation Various systems of recording the choreography of ballets in writing, including Benesh notation and Labanotation.

Nuance A slight or subtle difference which alters the meaning or effect.

O

Ouvert Open. When the feet are in an open position to the audience.

P

Parterre On the ground. As, for example, in *rond de jambe parterre*.

Pas Step. As, for example, in *pas de chat*.

Pas de bourrée Step of the bourrée. An old French dance refined and developed in classical ballet. It takes many forms but involves changing from one foot to the other several times.

Pas de chat Step of a cat. A jump in various forms that resembles the steps of a cat.

Pas de couru Running step. A traveling step composed of small running steps of varied forms.

Pas de deux A dance for two people.

Penché Leaning or tilted. As, for example, in *arabesque penchée* when the raised leg goes very high as the body leans forward.

Petit Small. As, for example, in *petit battement*.

Petit allegro The smaller jumps and traveling steps of *allegro*.

Petit battement Fast, small beats of the working leg in front of and behind the supporting leg.

Petite échappée A version of the jump *échappée sautée*, in which the legs are opened in the air before returning to the floor.

Pied Foot.

Pirouette Spinning top. A particular way of turning on one leg.

Placing The way the body is held according to the rules of classical ballet.

Plié Bent. A bending of the knee or knees.

Port de bras Carriage of the arms. A movement of the arms to and through various positions.

Pointe tendue Point stretched. When the leg is extended and stretched so that only the tips of the toes are on the floor.

Pointes, sur les On the points. The raising of the body onto the tip of the toes.

Pose A pose or particular position of classical ballet.

Préparation Preparation. The movement with which a dancer prepares to dance.

Principal A leading dancer in a ballet company.

R

Relevé Raised. A movement in which the body is raised up onto pointes or *demi-pointes*.

Retiré Withdrawn. When the toes of the working leg are raised from a closed position to a point just below the knee.

Révérence Curtsey. A curtsey or bow performed at the end of a class or performance.

Romantic ballet A style of ballet from the Romantic period in the first half of the 19th century.

Rond de jambe Circle of the leg. A circular movement of the leg.

Rosin A powder made from the sap of fir trees, which dancers put on the soles of their shoes to keep them from slipping.

S

Sauté Jumped. When a movement is performed with a jump as, for example, in *échappée sautée*.

Seconde, a la To the second. When the leg is in second position on the floor or in the air.

Simple Ordinary. As, for example, in *sissonne simple*.

Sissonne A special sort of jump from two feet that can be danced in many ways.

Sissonne simple A jump from two feet landing in *cou de pied devant* or *derrière*.

Soloist A dancer who performs alone.

Soutenu Sustained.

Spotting The movement of the head in pirouettes and other particular ways of turning.

Sur On or upon. As, for example, in *sur les pointes*.

Sur place On the spot.

Syncopation The stressing of the weak parts of the rhythm of a piece of music.

T

Tap dancing A style of dancing developed in North America, involving quick tapping of the toes and heels on the floor.

Temps levé Time raised. A hop on one foot.

Temps lié Time bound together. A sequence of movements connected together smoothly.

Tendu Stretched. As, for example, in *battement tendu*.

Tour en l'air Turn in the air.

Tournant, en Turning. When a step is done moving around.

Turnout The way the feet and legs should be turned out from the hip joints to give the freedom of movement necessary to perform the steps of classical ballet.

Index

Lara   Lisa   Robert   Anna   Darcey   Oliver   Nandita   Georgina   Alex   Elizabeth

Acknowledgments

Dorling Kindersley would like to thank the following people
for their help in the production of this book:

All the young dancers for giving up their spare time to be photographed for this book; Victoria Hewitt, Martin Howland, and Bennet Gartside for performing other dance forms for photography; Danielle Greenhalgh for providing an idea for a ballet story; all the staff at White Lodge, especially Carole Leicester for her help with the wardrobe; Amanda Jones at The Royal Ballet for her help and cooperation; Adrian Grater for his help with the Benesh notation; Dancia International of Drury Lane for lending clothes; Claire Bampton for editorial assistance; Susan St. Louis for design assistance; Kathy Lockley for Picture Research.

Darcey Bussell would like to thank:
Anthony Dowell for all his guidance in my career; my parents for always being there when I need help; and all the people who have trained and encouraged me so far.

Patricia Linton would like to thank:
Anatole Grigoriev for his support and help with placing the dancers for photography; Dame Merle Park, Rashna Homji-Jefferies, Shirley Grahame, Christine Beckley, and Janet Briggs for their comments on parts of the text; also, for their advice and comments: Carole Leicester on costumes, Ron Smedley and Bob Parker on American square dancing, William Ireland on Scottish dancing, Joy Ransley on Irish dancing, Bill Drysdale on tap and jazz, Ross McKim on contemporary dancing, Fred le Conte on set painting, and Guy Attew on musicals; Audrey Harman, the Royal Ballet School archivist; and finally Nicole Vlasto for checking the French.

Picture credits
key: B bottom; L left; R right; C center; T top.
Bridgeman Art Library: 49BL
Camera Press/Anthony Crickmay: 7BR, 40BL, 40R, 43, 53BR, 53L
Dee Conway: 55CL
English National Ballet: 49CR, 49TR
Nan Melville: 49TL. 49CL, 51TR, 57C, 58CR, 58CL; /Choreography by George Balanchine. © The George Balanchine Trust: 25C, 57TR
Rex Features: 54BL, 55CR
Linda Rich: 29TR, 35TR, 37T, 58BR, 60CL

Leslie E Spatt: 36C, 51TL, 56CL, 58CR, 59BL, 60BL; /Choreography by George Balanchine. Used by permission of Copyright Owner, Edward Bigelow: 50CL
Martha Swope Associates/Carol Rosegg: 22CL
Reg Wilson: 26TR, 29TR, 44C, 56TR, 57BR, 58C, 58TR, 59TC; /Choreography by George Balanchine. © The George Balanchine Trust: 57TL.

Every effort has been made to trace the copyright holders and we apologize in advance for any unintentional omissions. We would be pleased to insert the appropriate acknowledgment in any subsequent edition of this publication.

Back Flap Credit
Universal Pictorial Press: TL.

Additional DK photography: Andy Crawford